SAVED
by the
IRS

A TRUE STORY

SAVED
by the
IRS

Ken Jones

TATE PUBLISHING
AND ENTERPRISES, LLC

Published by Tate Publishing & Enterprises, LLC
127 E. Trade Center Terrace | Mustang, Oklahoma 73064 USA
1.888.361.9473 | www.tatepublishing.com

Tate Publishing is committed to excellence in the publishing industry. The company reflects the philosophy established by the founders, based on Psalm 68:11,
"The Lord gave the word and great was the company of those who published it."

Book design copyright © 2011 by Tate Publishing, LLC. All rights reserved.
Cover design by Shawn Collins
Interior design by Blake Brasor

Published in the United States of America

ISBN: 978-1-61862-680-6
Biography & Autobiography / Business
12.05.24

Dedication

To my Lord and Savior, Jesus Christ, and my two sons,
Kenny and Michael Jones

Acknowledgments

I want to thank the one man who made this book possible, David Aughtry, my attorney in Atlanta. David had no fear of the forces of evil—the IRS. I admired David for refusing to give me up on a silver platter as the IRS requested.

I dedicate this book to my beloved sons, Kenny and Michael, for all their love, devotion, and faith in me. Their love gave me what was necessary to survive all those difficult years. An inspiration I played a thousand times over in my mind was what my twenty-three-year-old son, Kenny, told me in 1988. It became my driving force to survive. "Daddy, only God can help us now."

As a believer in Him, I am so thankful for God placing Teresa in my life in 2009 to be my wife and help me write this inspirational story of the power of God.

Table of Contents

Prologue

This book has been written for several reasons. The biggest desire for me was to please God. I felt compelled by his spirit to chronicle this story to tell of God's strength and abundant love for us all and how he saved me. He is a forgiving and merciful God, and he laid it on my heart to share this private event in my life—not only to show his power and his forgiving nature full of abundant love but also because there may be people out there reading this story that have had similar situations and do not have God in their lives to help them. This will hopefully help you make a decision to allow God into your life. The decision to allow God to be a part of your life and to accept Jesus Christ as your Lord and Savior will truly be the best and most powerful decision for you and your loved ones, but most of all for your eternity.

Let me also add that throughout this true story, for the sake of clarity and brevity, I have referred to the Department of Treasury, Internal Revenue Service, as the IRS only. This story is based on the truth as I know it and as it happened to me in my life.

We all have sinned and fallen short of the glory of God, but the really great thing about God is that he never leaves us or forsakes us. In fact, you will see that I left God out of my life for a while. But God was always there for me, and when I once again made Him the most important part of my life, God gave me the strength and the faith to survive the biggest battle against the forces of evil, the IRS. God forgave me of my sins and helped me survive and obtain the victory that I needed to save my life, my business, and my family.

He is our creator, and God made us in his image to worship Him and to win souls to his kingdom. He is our living God, soon to return for his children. Praise be to his holy name!

> Blessed is the man who perseveres under trial, because once he has been approved, he will receive the crown of life which the Lord has promised to those who love Him.
>
> James 1:12

The Assault

This is a true story of what can happen to anyone, any-where, at any time in America. It just so happens it occurred in the small town of Macon, Georgia, which is known for a lot of history and home of Little Richard, Otis Redding, and home of Capricorn Records, Southern rock in the 1970s. You will see how God has placed me here with a reason and a purpose for it all. Everything can change in the blink of an eye, but do not worry—God never blinks.

> But, indeed, for this cause I have allowed you to remain, in order to show you My power, and in order to proclaim My name through all the earth.
>
> Exodus 9:16

This true story is on the Internet around the world. You can Google my name, James Kenneth Jones.

On Monday, October 20, 1986, at 10:30 a.m., I was in my office standing up behind my desk designing a full-page advertisement for the Macon Telegraph. I always designed and created my store ads for print and

TV for my well-established business known as Ken's Stereo Junction.

I founded the business with a thirty-thousand-dollar bank loan with my brother Harry in 1978. This day started out as normal work day, but all of a sudden, it became a day that changed my life forever.

In just five minutes, God brought what I thought was a powerful, invincible man to his knees. I looked up and I saw about twelve to fifteen well-dressed men and women walking through the store from my rear-office window. I thought to myself, Wow, how unusual is this on an early Monday morning to have this many customers in the store at one time?

Just as I noticed all the activity in the store, a Bibb County sheriff's deputy, a friend and customer of mine, was walking to my office with some other people. Deputy Curtis had visible tears streaming out of his eyes, and I had a gut feeling that something was terribly wrong. Seeing a grown man walking into my office crying was something that never had happened to me!

I asked Curtis, "What's the matter, and how can I help you?" He stepped backwards, and in walked a stocky white man wearing a white, summery short-sleeved shirt with red tie. His hair was gray and he appeared to be about sixty years old. He was accompanied by six men dressed in black suits with ties and white shirts. They walked in behind him, spacing themselves around the office in a military stance, while pulling back their jackets, revealing their pistols and badges of some sort.

While I was standing there looking at this short, stocky man, who had papers clutched in his hand and apparently was the only one not brandishing a weapon, he said, "Ken, I am Mr. Casteel, and I'm with the IRS. According to a statue number that I can't recall, you owe the IRS $948,164.90.

I said, "Where did you get those figures, Mr. Casteel?"

He replied to me very hatefully without blinking his eyes, "It doesn't matter!"

"Yes, it does matter!"

Bearing a smirk on his face, Mr. Casteel looked me directly in the eyes and said, "Ken, can you pay? You have five minutes, and we will take a check."

I had a feeling in the pit of my stomach like someone I loved very much had just died. I was deteriorating from within and feeling as if my insides had crumbled. "No, I cannot pay." I was in total shock, but an unexplainable peace and calm came over me. I did not know where those figures were coming from or what he was talking about.

I admit I was mesmerized, and it all seemed surreal. But looking back at that moment, I feel that it was God giving me that inner peace and calm that I especially needed.

Standing there with my mind whirling, and always being a positive thinker, I was trying to comprehend where in the world I would I get that kind of money. I was feeling intensely intimidated, which was a feeling I had never experienced in my entire adult life. While still standing staid behind my desk, I opened up my middle drawer just to give myself a chance to think.

As panic was obliterating my thoughts, I started to open up my middle drawer and was fumbling around in the drawer trying to buy some time to gather my thoughts. Then suddenly I heard all of their weapons being pulled out of their holsters. As I slowly looked up, I saw each of the government men pointing their weapons directly at my head.

I was shocked to see all of their reactions to me just trying to buy some time. All of their guns were drawn on me in synchronization as though I was some kind of fugitive serial killer just cornered and captured.

I looked at Mr. Casteel and said, "What are you people doing?"

"Ken, we know you were an Atlanta policeman, and we know you were an expert pistol marksman in your day. We also know you have a pistol license."

"Are you worried about me blowing my brains out, Mr. Casteel?"

"No, Ken, we are more worried about you blowing our brains out because of what we are about to do to you." Then Mr. Casteel asked me, "Where is your pistol?"

It's in my Corvette in front of the store." "You can have the pistol, but give us the bullets."

He and the six armed men followed me to my car. As we were walking out there, I saw a wrecker hooking up my red Corvette to haul it away. I told them, trying to avoid damage to the car, "I will give you the keys after I retrieve the gun for you."

When we returned inside the store, I asked Mr. Casteel, "What are you people doing right now to me and my family business?"

Mr. Casteel replied, "Ken, we're seizing everything you own, including your car. You can surrender your wife's Lincoln tomorrow, your son's car, both of your stores today, and your inventory, plus you must sell your home, and in addition, we have already seized ninety-four thousand dollars from your company checking account. Let's go to the C & S Bank and get the titles to your cars and all the cash in your safety deposit box with the US Marshals."

I told Mr. Casteel I didn't have any cash, but only old coins from the deceased brother of my wife, Grace. Grace's brother, Bill, had given us the coins before he had died of cancer at age forty-two, in 1980. When we entered the bank, all the employees including Jean Lindsey, the manager, already knew the IRS had been in the bank an hour earlier and had seized all of my assets. I could see the distain for the IRS in the eyes of Jean Lindsay. I asked Mr. Casteel not to take the old coins that amounted to only $500, but he did any way. The IRS has no shame.

After returning to the store, Mr. Casteel reached into my desk drawer and even took the roll postal stamps that I had in there and put them in his pocket. Mr. Casteel told me that the IRS never wanted me to return to my stores again after I left there that day. "That's why we are putting yellow tape around the entrances of both of your stores."

I looked at Mr. Casteel sternly in the eyes and asked him, "Do you mean to tell me you people can come in here and take everything I have worked so hard for all of my life without any proof, a hearing, or court proceedings?"

Mr. Casteel replied, "Yes, we can, and that is what we are doing right now."

Little did I know at the same time, the IRS had also invaded my store in Warner Robins (twenty-five miles south of Macon), where my brother Harry was working, just as they had entered and taken over the store in Macon. The IRS also had six armed men in black that came there and cornered my brother. Harry was behind the sales counter when they arrived. They flashed open their jackets to reveal their badges and weapons to him. These men stood in a military stance spaced around the sales counter and rudely told my brother to get out of the store.

Harry said, "Okay, but I have to go in the back office and get my jacket." Two armed men followed Harry into the office, and he asked them, "What is this about?" They told Harry to just get out, and Harry said, "Okay, okay!" Harry said they did not actually pull their weapons on him like they had on me. But he noticed some of their people had immediately started taking inventory. The IRS had a locksmith changing the locks on the doors and putting yellow tape around the building as Harry was leaving. They were in the process of closing down both stores.

As I was walking out of my store in a state of numbness, Mr. Casteel said, "Ken, do not talk bad about the

IRS. I don't want to hear of you saying anything bad about us, and none of this should ever be used in any kind of advertisement against us."

As I was numbly making my way out of the door, I could not believe that he had the nerve to even say that to me at that time.

In total disbelief and shock, I was repeating to myself over and over, "How could this happen in the land of the free—America?" Armed government men seizing everything a man has worked for all his life just like Nazi Germans did to the Jews in the thirties, but this was in America!

This is a historically true story that has been well documented on the Internet and in American and Russian law books. Little did I know how God was directing my life in a new direction and what it was going to take to get me to heed to God's call on my life.

> You have been severed from Christ, you who are seeking to be justified by law, you have fallen from grace.
>
> Galatians 5:4

Beginnings

Looking back now at age of sixty-seven, growing up poor was truly a blessing; as you see this horrific true story unfold, you will understand. God was preparing me all along to use what I call my *visionary mind* to mold the man I had to be later on in life against all odds and extreme adversity.

> If you slack in the day of distress, your strength
> is limited.
>
> Proverbs 24:10

I was born in Atlanta, Georgia, in 1944, to Christine Crowe Jones and Jimmy Jones. My parents got married on Christmas Day in 1942. Mother was a loving Christian woman with a heart of gold, and my daddy was a very emotional and physically abusive man. Neither of my parents had much of a formal education.

My mother quit school in the eighth grade and went to work as a waitress in downtown Atlanta. My daddy only finished the tenth grade and said he educated himself in the school of hard knocks. My daddy did have the gift of salesmanship, but what I remember the most about him was his abrupt anger and the emotional and physical abuse he inflicted on our whole family.

When I was at the tender age of five years old, my daddy, in a fit of anger one morning, took a glass plate and broke it over the back of my head. He said he did this because I was not eating my breakfast fast enough. We lived in a poor section of Atlanta about three miles south of the capitol.

That particular morning my teacher told me to go home because I was bleeding profusely from the back of my head where I had been struck with the plate.

The force of the blow to my head had cracked the bottom of my skull. We were too poor to go to the hospital, so by the grace of God my skull healed on its own. My skull grew outward at the site of the fracture, leaving a huge knot on the base of my skull that is visible today.

In those days there weren't any child protective services to report abuse to, so incidents like this went unreported.

I also remember as a child seeing my mother being beaten on the sofa in the three-room home where I lived with my parents. This trauma caused me to develop a stutter.

I was healed by God.

> But Jesus said, "Let the children alone, and do not hinder them from coming to Me, for the kingdom of heaven belongs to such as these."
>
> Matthew 19:14

Daddy would often say, "Are you going to make it?" I had no idea what he was talking about as a boy, not knowing that it was God's way of preparing me to be strong later on in life. What does not kill you really makes you stronger.

We grew to a family of seven and lived in a house with only four rooms till I was thirteen years old. I remember homeless men would knock on our door, and Mother would make sandwiches and give them water then send them on their way. As a young boy, we were very poor, but I never knew that we were poor because that was all I knew. I had never been around wealthy people. I had a wonderful and kind mother that loved me and my younger siblings and told us we were special all of the time. Life isn't fair, but it is still good.

The fact that my daddy was from a generation cursed with child abuse and a victim of child abuse himself made him an abusive father and husband. Daddy was born in 1921 and was given away by his mother to his grandmother in Leslie, Georgia. Daddy was born in that small South Georgia town, and his grandmother died when he was only eight years old. His mother never loved him and gave him away all of his life to strangers, so he took his physical and emotional abuse rages out on me since I was the oldest of five children.

Daddy had a habit of using fear on me and would emphasize this by putting his fist in my face, opening up his hand with his five fingers stretched out, and screaming, "I did not have a daddy for five minutes," which scared me as a small boy.

I got used to his fist being shoved in my face a lot and grew up without fear of anything or anyone. I had no idea why I was treated so badly, but I believe that was God's way for me to become a fighter. Daddy's generational curse of abuse from his mother would continue until I broke the cycle with my generation.

In those early years growing up, Daddy would say to me, "Kenneth, you will never amount to a hill of beans!" I asked my mother, "What does that mean, Mother that I will never amount to a hill of beans?" Mother replied to me, "Honey, don't worry about that, 'cause, Kenneth, he is just crazy!"

> Whoever receives one child like this in My name receives Me; and whoever receives Me, does not receive Me, but Him who sent Me.
>
> Mark 9:37

Ken at age eight

Daddy was a traveling salesman, so we all looked for-ward to Daddy leaving every week. He would often leave on Sunday nights, and we always dreaded him returning on Friday evenings.

God had his hand on my life and was working in my life even in those early years. Daddy met Pastor Jimmy Mayo by the grace of God, and that began to help change everything. We started attending the Washington Street Assembly of God Church, which later became the Assembly of God Tabernacle on Boulevard.

Daddy seemed to change for the better as Jesus started to be more a part of his life. Brother Mayo helped Daddy find the Lord, and that changed eve-rything for the better, but his past abuse caused him problems all his life. Daddy seemed a lot less violent after having Christ working on him, and it was a bless-ing for everyone in our family. I found the Lord when I was twelve years old and I grew strong in the light of his presence and had the peace I needed that God granted me in those difficult years.

Inbetweeners

Our family moved into the middle-class west end of Atlanta in 1960, and I attended Brown High School.

Daddy had a heart attack at the age of thirty-nine. I think mainly because he smoked and weighed 325 pounds. I was forced to work after school to help support the family when I was fifteen years old. I worked for tips at Colonial grocery store. I contributed about one hundred dollars a month to the support of my family, which helped supplement the Social Security check that Daddy received each month. Mother got a job as a waitress working for her uncle in downtown Atlanta to also help support our family of seven.

The Johnsons, who lived two doors down from us, had two sons, Steve and David. Steve and I were the same age and fast became buddies. The Johnsons had a cabin in the north Georgia mountains on a lake, and I thought they were rich. Mr. Johnson always treated me with respect and kindness.

For the first time in my life, I saw what a normal family was like when they invited me to their home. Before, I thought all families had turmoil, fussing, and a chaotic life the majority of time. Mr. Johnson was a good man, but their family clearly had a different value system from what I was used to in ours.

God was working on me even then, and I did not know or understand why I had been treated so badly all of my life. I wanted the same type of family life as the Johnsons were living.

One time, Steve was at my house and we were both eating hamburgers. Steve ate one burger. Daddy told me that he wanted fifty cents for Steve's hamburger. I paid the fifty cents, not letting Steve know how greedy my father was. So in a few minutes, Steve asked to have another hamburger, and I told him, "Steve, please, I can't afford it!"

Steve said, "Are you kidding?"

I said, "No! I have to pay for every hamburger that you eat!" This was another way that Daddy humiliated me in front of my friends. Steve left our home in total disbelief.

I know now that God was continually making me stronger for a day fifty years later. Today I buy my employees lunches about once a week, feeding up to twenty-five people in Macon and Warner Robins. My two sons have never asked why I buy lunches for the people I care about. But I do it because of the degrading circumstance of the fifty-cent hamburger to my best friend over fifty years ago.

I believe emphatically that God does work through others and was preparing me to be the strong man I would need to be later on in life. I felt blessed to see what a normal family life was supposed to be like through my time spent with the Johnsons.

I had a few friends in school but was a loner for the most part. I did not have the opportunity to play sports because I worked all the time. Every afternoon after school, and every Saturday, I worked to help feed our family.

Daddy always called life a rat race, and it was in his world. I saw life differently. I envisioned life as an opportunity. My goal was to get out on my own as soon as I could. I believed, even in those early years, that being an American was very special.

I had a fifth-grade teacher Miss Toleson who told me that America was a land of opportunity, and a land of special rights like no other country in the world. For the first time in my life I was told about how being an American was very special and I could even become the President of the United States.

My thoughts of my fifth grade teacher came to me as I was driving home from the assault and unlawful seizure by the IRS with armed government men seizing all of my assets without due process of the law on that dreadful day.

I remembered my childhood days when my fifth-grade schoolteacher that taught me the American constitutional rights. I started asking myself, what has become of America's fundamental foundation? Is the US government above our constitutional laws?

I got to thinking if the US government can do this to me, then how long can the US Government do this to anyone they choose! What has happened to the American spirit if you have a government agency that is above the law of the land?

I made average grades. I really had no interest and was bored in high school and didn't know why until I took an IQ test and discovered that I had an IQ of 146. I became the first generation in many from my family to graduate from high school. My mother was so proud of me,

My passion was strong to get out of our home and away from my daddy. I believed if hard work would get me there, then someday, somehow, I would be the man who would not have to answer to anyone. I dreamed of being somebody, and I would not be denied that. I always prayed to be in the will of God. Just think about it, how can you go wrong if you are in the will of God?

I was determined not to be like my daddy. I saw him as a fat, greedy, and abusive man. I was determined to break the generational curse of abuse. The more that daddy tried to destroy my ego and self-esteem, the stronger I got. Little did I know at that time that is was God's way of preparing me for the seven-year fight of my life with the forces of evil, the IRS.

God continued to make me stronger because this is the power in all of us that he blesses us with. I grew up fast and trusted no one but my mother. I listened to older people growing up for wisdom. The book of Proverbs is my favorite book in the Bible for all the wisdom it has in it. There is great power in prayer when you pray in the name of Jesus. If God is in your heart, you will have the power.

I found this secret out early in my life. I knew I had a gift that few people know of that I call the visionary mind. This power served me well all my life, and I have a chapter about this awesome power God gave us all.

The Holy Bible is full of visionary minds such as Moses and Solomon. Jesus said, "The Kingdom of God is within you."

I feel that the power of wisdom, or permanent success, comes from within, because the mind is the cause and the means that can bring you to either side. Your mind is the most powerful organ that God created, and it is the most active organ, both the conscious and subconscious mind. What you think is what you get, "As a man thinketh." You can think healthy or sick according to your thoughts or images that you let control your mind. Do not let your thoughts be of disease and decay. Always be thinking about ways to improve your health and habits. Disease and fear are not sent from God. God gave us a twenty-four-hour powerhouse that will amaze you with what powers you have that you never knew about. I will address this more thoroughly later in the book.

> And all things you ask in prayer, believing, you shall receive.
>
> Matthew 21:22

When I graduated in 1962, a teacher I did not know wrote a caption under my name in my 1962 Brown High School yearbook. She wrote: "I am myself my own commander."

I ask how she knew twenty years ahead what I was going to be like. Did she have the visionary mind?

> For God has not given us a spirit of timidity, but of power and love and discipline.
>
> 2Timonthy 1:7

"I am myself my own commander"

One day I went to the Assembly of God Tabernacle Church on Boulevard. I met Grace Ann Ellington on a blind date at age nineteen. We hit it off from the start because we both had the same values and lived with humble means. I adored her mother, Ruby, a great woman of God, and she had a wonderful sister named Jane.

Grace and I dated, and in those days when you graduated from high school it was like the movie Peggy Sue Got Married—you dated and then married. On May 16, 1964, just before Grace graduated, we were married at Assembly of God Tabernacle by Jerry Bray.

Grace's mother was a true blessing to me that turned out to be a loving mother-in-law to me for forty-seven years. She was always so kind to me.

> For this cause a man shall leave his father and his mother, and shall cleave to his wife: and they shall become one flesh.
>
> Genesis 2:24

When I married Grace at the young age of twenty, I cared for Grace, and it got me away from Daddy and all the turmoil. We were too poor to go on a honeymoon. Daddy threatened to stop the wedding because he felt he was losing a son, but he had lost me years before to abuse.

Grace and I rented a furnished apartment, and I got some part-time jobs and applied to be an Atlanta policeman.

Two months after Grace and I married, tragedy hit our family when my thirteen-year-old sister Shirley fell out of a tree by accident. She had a severe head injury and died. My mother grieved herself to death and developed breast cancer and died two years later at the age of forty-two. She went to be with the Lord on July 13, 1966. That was the day our family died, for Mother was the glue that held the family together.

I do know there is an afterlife because mother's father died in an Alabama hospital five days before mother passed on. No one told her of his passing, because she was so sick. Just before Mother died, she looked up to the corner of the room and said, "Daddy, what are you doing here?" We were all shocked that she had seen her daddy, who had passed away five days earlier.

I sometimes feel cheated losing both Mother and Shirley when I was so young. One verse from the Bible that gives me some relief from the grief when I think of our loss is this:

> ...and if children, heirs also, heirs of God and fellow heirs with Christ, if indeed we suffer with Him in order that we may also be glorified with Him. For I consider that the sufferings of this present time are not worthy to be compared with the glory that is to be revealed to us.
>
> Romans 8:17-18

I truly believe the answer to every problem mankind has or will ever have is in the Holy Bible.

I was approved to become a policeman, and they assigned me to office duty from 11:00 p.m. till 7:00 a.m. I took this shift so I could work more jobs in the daytime to make extra money to support my family, because I did not want Grace to work. I believe early years are important for the mother and child to be together.

As an Atlanta policeman I noticed a freckle-faced black man that came around on my eleven p.m. to seven a.m. shift when I had office duties before I went to the police academy. He was always very friendly, and we would talk some while I answered calls from people the operators could not help. I am not sure of his duties at the station, but I saw him often.

Who would have ever guessed that twenty-five years later, that same man would become very famous Atlanta policeman, and once again we would cross paths under very different circumstances? I will reveal who he was later in the book. He has gotten a second chance in life today, just as I did.

I worked as an Atlanta policeman for three years. I loved the work and enjoyed the respect it brought to me. But you just don't make enough money to support a family without extra jobs on the side. So I started looking around for something that would take less hours and where I would be paid for results.

I thought in my heart, "God will bring to judgment both the righteous and the wicked, for there will be a time for every activity, a time for every deed" (Ecclesiastes 3:17).

A Fork in the Road

A plan in the heart of a man is like deep water.
But a man of understanding draws it out.

Proverbs 20:5

Before turning in my resignation to the police department, I had secured an offer for another job with a bakery company. I left the police department and worked for the bakery for two years. The vending route with the bakery came to an end because it was not profitable for them, but they offered me another job with them. I had accepted the continuation of employment with them, but during this time, I had spoken to a Mr. Groover with Gulf Life Insurance about the possibility of working for them selling life and health insurance.

I talked with Mr. Groover, the manager of Gulf Life, for about thirty minutes two weeks prior about working for Gulf Life. I went by to see Mr. Groover again even though I had made a commitment for another job. But the Holy Spirit of God kept leading me in my heart and mind to go meet with him strictly as a courtesy to tell him no to the job offer. But little did I know that it was truly God's hand on me and changing the fork in the road of my life's path that day. Thank God that I listened to the Holy Spirit's guidance.

I felt a real connection with Mr. Groover. Mr. Groover had gray hair and a wonderful smile, and before I knew it, we had talked for three hours. Toward the end of our conversation he said, "Kenneth, I believe you can be a great man for Gulf Life."

So I replied excitedly, "Okay!"

I know it sounds like Forest Gump, but that is how God changed my entire life. With that change in direction, many people's lives were changed. What I thought would be a five-minute chat had turned into a three hour conversation.

The fact is I did not have a clue about insurance. I did not own life insurance or believe in life insurance when I started to work for Gulf Life.

But God, in all his glory, changed so many lives through Mr. Sol Groover, a real man of God, forty-two years ago. That one decision changed lives as to who my two sons married, my grandchildren, because I later moved to Macon. My move began my rags-to-riches story and later my downfall and redemption through the power of God once again changing me and my life. Mr. Groover knew of my problems with the IRS but never knew the outcome; or maybe he does! I am sure he is in glory land! Praise God!

In sales as an agent, I went from last to third place the first year, and by the third year I was number one in the district and number fifteen in the company out of eight hundred agents. I was getting recognition from

Mr. Groover every week to Grace with personal letters and on the weekly sales bulletin to all the sales force.

In my opinion, people work on only two motives and those are fear and praise.

I was twenty-five years old, and it doesn't make a difference where one lives or works, everyone wants to feel noticed, respected, and valued in life. I found my place in life for then, and I loved working and getting paid for results. I found out that I loved the thrill of winning and the recognition that came with it. I was getting what my daddy denied me all of my life, praise.

> And we know that God causes all things work together for good to those who love God, to those who are the called according to His purpose.
>
> Romans 8:28

A New Direction By God

But it is a spirit in man, and the breath of the Almighty gives them understanding.

Job 32:8

After just three years, the home office of Gulf Life in Jacksonville, Florida, took notice and wanted to promote me to staff manager. I was unstoppable and wanted to go higher and prove myself to be the best there was at the next level. I was going to be a lot more than what my daddy had continuously pounded in my head my entire childhood: "You will never amount to be a hill of beans."

I always listened to my inner spirit. I like to call it my visionary mind. The visionary mind is real, and it is a gift from God. In fact, from the day you are born, I believe that you have all of your life experiences stored in your mind forever.

I took on a staff of five agents in Macon, Georgia, when I was only twenty-eight years old. I was known as the "city slicker" from Atlanta and was the youngest there. I took on a staff that was close to the bottom in the company in 1972. Gene Copeland, the district manager, was a real leader and taught me a great deal of management skills.

I will always be grateful for all Gene gave me in support. He was a great communicator. He had a way to get to people to give their all and to be the best at what they were doing. Gene loved to see people grow and prosper, and all true leaders have that quality.

It was tough, for Grace and me, because we did not know a soul in Macon, Georgia. We moved there in 1972 and purchased an old house at 3951 Ridge Avenue from the Crockett estate originally built in 1911, in north Macon.

We soon started a daycare center at our home for Grace. This was what she wanted, and it was a great success. Grace had a natural talent and loved babies, and the mothers sensed this. We started out with just one child, and it grew to fifteen in just six months.

We added on to the back of the house to accommodate forty children, which it had grown to in three years. Looking back, Grace and I were building a wonderful life together in a Leave It to Beaver neighborhood, never knowing it was one of the best times of our lives.

In three years I became the number one staff manager out of 180 staffs for the entire company. Gene Copeland won the coveted District of the Year award. As a result, Gene was promoted to vice president of Gulf Life, and I was promoted to manager of the

Macon District. At the age of thirty-two, in 1976, I was the youngest manager in the history of Gulf Life. With my rise within the company, I always said, "It is the man, not the land." I proved it with my positions as a salesman and as a staff manager.

I sensed something was wrong after two years as manager. I did not know what it was with Gene, but the Macon district was number five out of forty-eight districts. This still was not good enough for Gene Copeland, and I did not know why. Gene would not let up on me. I did not work on fear, and Gene did not know that fact about me. I found out later that Gene's boss wanted the district for his son-in-law, of course he failed.

I am not one to take anything off of anyone as a byproduct of the abuse from my daddy. I just quit and went home to Grace and cried because I had put my heart and soul into the company for nine years.

Here again, God was working in my life. When I quit, I told Gene Copeland, "Gene, I don't know what I'll do, but I guarantee you one thing, I will be a millionaire in five years." For four months I just drifted and prayed a lot. I prayed to make peace with my past so it would not mess up my present. Life is too short to waste time hating anyone or anything.

One day I saw an AD in the Macon Telegraph Newspaper about a stereo and sewing center franchise out of Dallas, Texas. I called, and they said I could talk to the owners and to bring a ten-thousand-dollar cashier's check. So my brother Harry and I went on our merry way to Dallas, Texas, to check them out in May of 1978.

I caught the franchiser and their dealers telling different stories, and some outright lied on their sales figures. We went back that night to the hotel, and I called Grace. Grace had always been my biggest supporter, and she said, "You're just as smart as anybody, so keep the money and do it yourself." So Harry and I took the next flight back to Atlanta early in the morning.

That weekend, Harry, his wife Kim, Grace, and I were just kidding around and came up with a name for the new stereo store. Grace named the store Ken's Stereo Junction. So the new adventure was born, my new company, and we opened it on June 23, 1978. The visionary mind that God gave me was beginning to work again.

> Blessed be God, who has not turned away my prayer, nor his loving kindness from me.
>
> Psalms 66:20

The Almighty Dollar

Where there is no vision, the people are unre-
strained. But happy is he that keeps the law.

Proverbs 29:18

I have always felt the reason most folks do not go far
in life is because they sidestep opportunity all the while
holding hands with procrastination.

For the first location of Ken's Stereo Junction, I
rented a sixteen-hundred-square-foot retail space in
the Summit Center, next to Hancock Fabrics, across
from the Macon Mall. The space I rented was only fifteen feet wide.

I borrowed $30,000 from C&S Bank, and they told
me that I had a 10 percent chance of succeeding with
this endeavor. It is failure that is easy, for success is
always tough. Failure never entered my visionary mind!

A very interesting fact is that neither Harry nor I
knew anything about the hi-fi or stereo business. I just
prayed and plugged into the visionary mind that God
gave me, simple but very true! I wanted the store to be
a fun place to shop for stereos, just that simple.

I found a guy who made funny and creative commercials for radio advertising in 1978. I bought his "Don't Be a Duck" campaign, which we have used for thirty-four years. He did all of the radio spots for the "Don't Be a Duck" advertising campaign.

In a year, we were a household name in middle Georgia. Even Georgia Governor Sonny Perdue quoted one of our commercials at a Cherry Blossom event a few years back when I saw him in Macon.

Ken's Stereo Junction was the first to use funny commercials on the radio in our area. We were also the first, to my knowledge, to offer free installation on car stereos in the country. People would come to the store just to see who was so outrageous to run such funny commercials.

In 1980, we built the new Ken's Stereo Junction close to our initial location across from the Macon Mall. The building was freestanding with 6,500 square feet that looked like a train station.

Ken's Stereo Junction with the duck logo became known all over the seventy-mile area and was making me a famous businessman.

How blessed is the man who finds wisdom, and the man who gains understanding.

Proverbs 3:13

One day while in the grocery store, I noticed people in new Cadillac's using strange-looking paper for money. I asked the cashier what was that, and she told me it was food stamps.

I saw this happening a lot and asked myself, "Why should I work twelve to fourteen hours a day while others are getting free money and driving new Cadillac's?" Even President Reagan mentioned this in 1983 in a speech.

After this revelation and seeing this apparent abuse of our government subsidies, that was when I started to skim money from the daycare center and my stereo store business in 1980.

Skimming is when you take money from your own business and don't pay taxes on it. I want to make it clear it was not out of greed. I take full responsibility for my actions, and I paid a heavy price for this sin.

> Render therefore to all their due: *taxes* to whom *taxes* [are due], customs to whom customs, fear to whom fear, honor to whom honor.
>
> Romans 13:7

There is a lot of truth to the old saying, *the harder I work, the luckier I get.* I worked harder, and in 1984 I built a good sales team. I built and opened a replica store and rental building on the same property in Warner Robins, Georgia, about twenty-five miles south of Macon and the home of Robins AFB.

While I was working so hard, I let the most important part out of my life go away—God and Jesus Christ, my Lord and Savior. Grace and I drifted apart, and the money became our God.

Grace and I traveled to Greece, Egypt, and a cruise down the Nile River, the Holy Lands and even the Playboy Mansion in the 1980s era. All of these travels were perks from Marantz, a vendor for our stores, because we had become one of their top dealers in America.

The fact remained Grace and I were both miserable together. We had all this world had to offer materially, but something was missing, and it was God and Jesus in our lives. We did not have the inner peace that only the Lord can give you. We did know the difference because we were raised in a Christian church environment. Life without God had no purpose and therefore did not contain the inner peace we all need so much from God.

Happiness has to come from within, and it only comes through having Jesus Christ in your heart and life. The next part of happiness is derived from giving to others. Being the head of the household I had failed my family as stated in the Bible. I had sinned by turning my back on God and putting money and material things in His place and soon my world would fall apart.

> For the love of money is a root **of** all kinds of evil. Some people, eager for money, have wandered from the faith and pierced themselves with many griefs.
>
> 1 Timothy 6:10

I remember Pastor Steve Johnson preaching one Sunday. He really rang my bell when he said, "Sin will cost you more that you ever would imagine, and that there is a point of no return with sin!" He is a great man of God, and I have written this quote he made in my Bible today as a constant reminder of how Satan can mislead and consume you.

There is no replacement for the beliefs and faith that I was taught growing up in the old days. When we first got married we were poor, but God was part of our lives. But at this juncture in our lives, Grace and I were far apart from God and no longer in love with each other.

We built a home on four acres that I named Woodcrest Manor Estate, with a swimming pool, pool house, and three-car garage. We owned a Jalpa Lamborghini, Mercedes convertible, and two prosperous electronic stores. We basically bought anything we wanted. But we were unhappy, and the Bible is clear on what we had done to ourselves. Life is all about choices. I was consumed by bad choices.

> Do not love the world, nor the things of the world. If anyone loves the world, the love of the Father is not in him.
>
> 1 John 2:15

I was notified in 1984, via mail, that a regular civil audit was being conducted by the IRS. I was using a very good accountant, Billy Lamb, whom I trusted. I thought nothing of the civil audit, even though I had been skimming money from the company and day care center for four years.

I had justified the skimming in my mind, but it was of no concern to me now at all in my mind as I had already justified these actions within myself. I was ensnared in the devil's trap of destruction that he sets for all of us.

I did not have a clue that a criminal investigation had begun in 1982 by the IRS. I was only led to believe that I was under a normal civil audit. I never received any kind of notification that my civil audit had been turned into a criminal audit, by the IRS. I was totally in the dark. Having said all of that, I was taught in school that without laws there would be no society, only anarchy.

I was brainwashed to believe that our government stands for justice for all. I was ignorant and naive to believe our government was honest.

I truly believed in the principles represented by our founding fathers. I had no idea that the IRS was corrupt to the bone and this was only the beginning of an outright attack on me and my rights as an American, and these were supposedly protected by a Constitution and a Bill of Rights.

Jeopardy
Assessment

For wisdom is protection just as money is protection. But the advantage of knowledge is that wisdom preserves the lives of its possessors.

Ecclesiastes 7:12

This is the definition of Jeopardy Assessment:

This is an assessment made by the IRS of the additional tax owed by a taxpayer who underpaid without resorting to the usual review procedures because the taxing officer believes that delay may jeopardize collection of the claim. The deficiency is assessed immediately and it includes additional amounts, additions to tax, and interest. The assessment is made for a prior year where the filing date, including extensions, has passed. The legal authority for jeopardy assessments is: IRC 6861 for income, estate, gift, and certain excise taxes; IRC 6862 for taxes other than income, estate, gift and certain excise taxes; and IRC 6867 for "Possessor of Cash."

Jeopardy assessments of tax are to be used sparingly. They are to be reasonable, appropriate, and limited to amounts which can be expected to protect the government. All jeopardy assessments have a common characteristic: prior to assessment, a determination is made that collection will be endangered if regular assessment and collection procedures are followed. The mere fact that a taxpayer is the subject of a special fraud investigation is not sufficient grounds for a jeopardy assessment. When it is determined that a taxpayer has little or no assets to offset the assessments, jeopardy assessment will generally not be pursued. Each jeopardy assessment must receive the personal approval of the area director.

Question: How would you move two electronic stores and a four-acre estate out of America?

The facts are that on October 20, 1986, US Marshalls from Atlanta, Columbus, and Macon, Georgia, came by force and took all material assets I owned.

The wisdom I gained is that we cannot trust the people we trust with enforcement of the tax laws. I did things I should not have done and paid the highest price for my sins.

From day one, the IRS investigators were a fraud. IRS Criminal Agent Gary Schwab started a concealed criminal investigation of me when he saw a full-page feature article about my home in the Macon paper. For eighteen months, he and IRS Criminal Investigator Agent Kathy Cunard conducted that secret investigation without ever telling me or anyone else about it.

This shows the beginning pattern of corruption of the IRS involving me, and then the seizure happened.

I think one of the most ironic parts of this entire four-year criminal investigation, prior to the illegal seizure in 1986, was that I was never read my Miranda rights! Yes, it is true. Shame on CID Investigator Gary Schwab and the IRS.

If you look at the definition of the Miranda rights on Wikipedia, you will see as follows:

> The Miranda warning (also referred to as Miranda rights) is a warning that is required to be given by police in the United States to criminal suspects in police custody (or in a custodial interrogation) before they are interrogated to inform them about their constitutional rights. In *Miranda v. Arizona*, the Supreme Court of the United States held that an elicited incriminating statement by a suspect will not constitute admissible evidence unless the suspect was informed of the right to decline to make self-incriminatory statements and the right to legal counsel (hence the so-called "Miranda rights"), and makes a knowing, intelligent and voluntary waiver of those rights. The Miranda warning is not a condition of detention, but rather a safeguard against self-incrimination; as a result, if law enforcement officials decline to offer a

> Miranda warning to an individual in their cus-
> tody, they may still interrogate that person and
> act upon the knowledge gained, but may not
> use that person's statements to incriminate him
> or her in a criminal trial.
>
> "Miranda Rights," *Wikipedia*, last modified
> November 23, 2011, http://en.wikipedia.org/
> wiki/Miranda_rights.

According to the filing papers, the IRS placed liens on my property on October 17, 1986. These liens were filed just three days prior to the assault. In fact, I did not receive any paperwork at all concerning the liens filed until two days after the seizure of all of my properties, businesses and cars, et cetera.

In all reality, the assault was not necessary because there was absolutely no way to sell my stores and home with federal liens levied against all of them. So I have to ask, after four years of an illegal criminal investigation, why did the IRS take every material thing I owned? They forced me to sell my rental property in Warner Robins, my home. I also had to relinquish the titles to my Corvette and Lincoln and sell both of them two days before Christmas in front of the IRS office. In addition to those items being sold they also took $94,000 from my business account. And as stated in the definition of Jeopardy Assessment, it is supposed to be reasonable, appropriately handled as to the amounts owed to the government, and they are supposed to know that their proceeds are in danger of being taken away, but I had absolutely no way to leave the country or anything like that as my business and home were in Macon. I also did not have the assets to go anywhere else.

One thing I feel like I really need to point out after all of those things listed in the previous paragraph happened and this was all done and never explained to me how this figure they claimed I owed on taxes was calculated, and furthermore, Mr. Casteel had stated to me, "It doesn't matter!" All of this was done without any kind of hearing or court procedure. I had absolutely no rights! Since the IRS has absolute power, he was right. It did not matter.

So this is America, and the question you have to ask yourself, can the IRS do this to me?

Of course, the answer is yes they can. There have been countless Americans that have committed suicide over the IRS corruption such as mine, and it has been documented. With the IRS having absolute power over everyone, this is why they must be abolished!

One of the most current IRS-related suicides in national news happened in Austin, Texas, on February 10, 2010. A fifty-three-year-old business man flew his plane into the IRS headquarters there because he had lost all hope of ever surviving his IRS battle. His final statement was, "I know I'm hardly the first one to decide I have had all I can stand." This is a tragedy.

This situation is so sad, for he lost his life, and an IRS agent's life was lost as well. I feel for both families, as they will never be the same. He was known as a mild-mannered man by his friends according to the news story. The news story online states he had been in a battle with the IRS for ten years. He had lost his retirement funds and $40,000 in savings. This insane action was taken because this man had lost all hope of ever getting his IRS issues resolved. I know in my case most people did not care; they were just glad it was not them! The IRS's greatest weapon is fear. America was founded as a republic of the people, by the people, for the people, and in my opinion I do not think we should have to fear our government. The Fair Tax system would stop the fear factor of the IRS.

Does the German Gestapo come to mind in the days of Hitler? But this is in America? Right?

An hour into the assault by the IRS, I thought of calling Jay Hawkins, my tax attorney. Jay had been handling my civil audit for about two years. Jay was from an old-school Macon family and was very conservative, plus he is a just and honest man. Jay's communications had mostly been with civil IRS auditor Bonnie Waldrep.

Jay walked into my store the day of the seizure in 1986 after I called him. I asked him, "Can the IRS come in my business and take everything I own and get away with it?"

Jay's answers were scary. He said, "Yes, unfortunately, Yes!"

I started to ask more questions, and he told me that was not the place to talk and to come by his office the next day.

While I was in the store, my eighteen-year-old son, Michael, who had just graduated from Riverside Military Academy in Gainesville, Georgia, with hon-

Saved by the IRS

ors, drove up in his new 1986 Camaro. The Camaro was a gift I had promised upon graduation, which I purchased for him. Michael came running into the store in a panic and said, "Daddy, Daddy, those people just stole my car!"

When Michael came bursting into the store, I was standing next to IRS criminal investigator Gary Schwab. Mr. Schwab is a huge man standing about six-foot-five and weighing about three hundred pounds. Schwab was leaning on the service counter, looking like a cat that had just eaten a mouse. He seemed to be enjoying destroying me and taking my business away from me by force with armed government men.

Schwab said something to my son Michael, "Watch it, boy!" and he grabbed Michael by the arm.

I was about six feet from Schwab, and I looked straight into his eyes with apparent real anger and said, "Schwab, You can do what you want to me, but do not ever bother my family. Did you get that?"

Schwab said, "I consider that a threat!" He then let go of Michaels arm.

I replied to him, "No, Schwab, that is a promise!" Schwab looked scared and intimidated and looked away. I meant every word. You don't fool with my family.

My mind was still in a daze as I drove home in a twelve-year-old cargo van that the IRS did not know the store owned. When I got home, Grace, a few of our employees, Harry, and our sons Kenny and Michael were all there. They were all looking to me for answers, and I told them I had not paid all of my taxes. I also told them that I did not know what was next and how very sorry I was. I told all of them to look for another job and to apply for unemployment.

That undoubtedly was one of the longest days in my life. I called Mother (Grace's mother, Ruby) in Gastonia, North Carolina, that night, and Ruby told me to hold my head up high, for I was a good man and a child of the King. I had not heard that for a long time, and it made me realize how much I needed God back in my life and his intervention and direction for me in this whole situation.

IRS seizes Macon man's stores in Robins, Macon

By Joseph Palmer
Macon Telegraph and News

The Internal Revenue Service seized Ken's Stereo Junction stores in Macon and Warner Robins Monday and issued a claim against the owner's plush Macon home.

Les Witmer, an IRS spokesman in Atlanta, said the action was taken because the stores' owner — James Kenneth Jones — owes five years' worth of federal income taxes "in excess of $750,000." Revenue officers seized the businesses between 11 a.m. and 2 p.m.

Jones has an unlisted telephone number and could not be reached for comment Monday night.

A red and white notice posted on the front door of Jones' stereo business at 3677 Mercer University Drive reads: "Warning: This property has been seized for nonpayment of internal revenue taxes due from Ken's ... Stereo Junc-

tion as nominee of James Kenneth Jones, 125 Woodcrest Dr., Macon, by virtue of levy issued by the District Director of Internal Revenue." Jones' other stereo shop is located at 2040 Watson Blvd. in Warner Robins.

Witmer said the federal tax liens are on file at the Bibb County and Houston County courthouses.

"WE SEIZED THE business, the property and liens have been filed against Jones," Witmer said. "Also a lien was filed against his personal residence in Macon."

Witmer could not give more explicit details about the action because he was contacted at home after regular business hours and did not have access to the documents. But he was able to confirm that the liens filed amounted to more than $750,000.

(See SEIZE, page 8A)

The next day, the IRS seizure of my stores was headlined on the front page of the Macon Telegraph. My uncle Eric who lived in Waycross, Georgia, called me and said it was in his newspaper. I was on local television news. The IRS had a lot of power to pollute the media so they could justify what they had done to me, even though it was illegal from day one.

The following day, having been a member of the Riverside Optimist Club fox six years, I decided to attend our monthly meeting. Most of the guys were acting like they did not know me and the others were only acting polite.

So I just got up and said, "I guess you guys heard what happened to me, and the fact is I did not pay all of my taxes. I am in trouble and do not know where it is going, and I will resign if you guys want me to." The guys were then all very friendly. All of them wished me the best and hoped that it would work out for me. Once I had acknowledged my sin, they accepted me and were behind me 100 percent.

In 1985, I donated a $65,000 sound system at the request of Dr. Kirby Godsey, President of Mercer University in Macon to the renovation of the historic Grand Opera House, built in 1884. Dr. Godsey is a great man of vision to save this historic landmark that had seen the likes of Houdini, Ben Hurr, and all of the greats of the 1920s era. The building has perfect acoustics and it architecturally an awesome building. A luncheon was given in my honor because I was the single largest donor to the renovation of the project. Since I was serving on the Board of Directors, I offered to resign and they refused, but I did anyway. I did not want to put shame on Dr. Godsey, but this proves that it was not all about greed on my part.

About five days after the assault, a vendor in California called me and said that he had read about me in their newspaper. I had no idea that the US Government had sent my case on the Associated Press around America until then. I guess the IRS wanted to make me an example, and at that time, I had no idea that the IRS had been investigating me for four years behind my back.

In the meantime, a friend of mine loaned me a Volkswagen Jetta to drive. So, I went to my Uncle Eric's home in Waycross, Georgia (one hundred miles south of Macon), to see if he would say that I had received the money that taxes were not paid on from my daddy. Eric said yes, but I noticed that everything I said to him, he was repeating it, over and over to himself.

So, I asked Aunt Jean, "Why is Uncle Eric repeating everything I tell him, over and over, like a parrot?"

She said, "I think he is getting Alzheimer's." So I said wow to myself and left in deep despair.

Driving back to Macon, my pistol was under the front seat, and I was drinking a six pack of beer. I drove into a parking lot of a convenience store and just sat there grieving over the mess I had created.

Old Satan seems to be always around when you are at the weakest points in life. Thank God I knew this fact, because I was taught in my church that Satan always comes to seek and destroy you and everything in your life.

Satan put the thought in my mind that I could end it all right there in Alma, Georgia. I was very confused and was experiencing deep depression knowing that all of my options were running out.

Satan was telling me to kill myself over and over, but Jesus was telling me I was special and a child of the King! Satan wants you to feel defeated and conquered when God has actually already conquered the battles for you.

I thought that if I did kill myself, then everyone would believe all of the rumors that the IRS was spreading around about me being involved in drugs. With those thoughts in my head, I knew that my family, whom I loved so much, would lose it all and it would mean that the forces of evil, the IRS, would win.

I had been a winner all my life, and I decided right then and there in Alma, Georgia, that I would turn this over to God and Jesus Christ, my Lord and Savior, entirely. I would fight till the day I died, and I would survive this attack. I would do all of this with God's help. I realized right then and there that God was the only way to salvage this situation I had brought on myself, my family, and my business.

I told myself that I could survive and that I would give God all the glory. For God knew me from the womb, and I have been blessed with a visionary mind and there will be "Victory in Jesus," just like the song I sang in church as a boy.

I praise God almighty that Satan lost to the King of kings that day, again! I did not know how long it would take to defeat the most powerful forces of evil, the IRS, but survive I would, and God would see me through it all!

I have also found out some other interesting facts about the escapades that the IRS had pulled. One instance was during late 1985 when Grace's seventy-three-year-old mother Ruby called me from her modest shotgun-style home.

Ruby was well respected and loved by everyone that lived in Gastonia, North Carolina. She told me that two people with the IRS had come to her modest home. They showed her their badges and identified themselves as IRS agents.

Ruby said she told the man and woman, who were criminal investigators Schwab and Cunard, that I was a good provider for Grace Ann and the two boys and could not be a better son-in-law and that she knew that I loved the Lord.

She said they also asked her if she had given me any money, and she said no. She told them that I was very smart, a fine man, and that I worked very hard and she was living on social security. Ruby told me they just got up and did not say a word and left. I guess Schwab and Cunard were upset because they had wasted a six-hundred-mile trip and did not want to hear anything good about me.

About two weeks later, Joan Ellington, my sister-in-law called Grace from Longview, Texas, and told Grace that the CID investigators Schwab and Cunard came to her home. Schwab and Cunard were there asking her the same questions as they had Ruby. Joan told them the same thing about me. She said they were very rude to her and just got up and left because this time they had wasted a two-thousand-mile trip with the same end results: I was a good man. I have often wondered why they were not smart enough to just pick up the phone and call these relatives rather than waste taxpayer dollars going on two separate long trips to question them.

So in 1987, by chance, I ran across my old boss Gene Copeland of Gulf Life in Macon. Gene told me that an IRS man by the name of Schwab had called him. The first question he asked Gene was, "How much money did Ken Jones steal from Gulf Life as manager in Macon?"

Gene told him that I had never stolen a penny. He further told him that "Ken Jones had quit Gulf Life, and we tried our best to get him back. In fact that he was one of the best managers that Gulf Life had ever had."

He told me that before he could finish the sentence that the IRS man hung up on him. It is clear that Schwab did not want to hear that I was a good manager. The IRS is all about destroying a person, so why put something good in their assessment for the judge?

> My brethern, "if any among you strays from the truth, and one turns him back, let him know that he who turns a sinner from the error of his way will save his soul from death, and will cover a multitude of sins.
>
> James 19:20

Cash Stash

He who loves money will not be satisfied with money, nor he who loves abundance with its income. This too is vanity.

Ecclesiastes 5:10

The week of the seizure, October 1986, I had no doubt the IRS knew I had some cash, because I had withdrawn fifty-seven thousand dollars from the bank in September. This was upon the advice of my criminal attorney. He had also told me to put my home up for sale so we would have money to pay any taxes we owed. This was public knowledge, as we had placed a for-sale sign in our front yard. He also told me to take my savings out of the bank so I would have money to pay my attorney's fees. All of these actions were based on my criminal attorney's advice.

I had a little cash stashed at home, but that was it. So not knowing what the IRS would be up to next, I definitely was feeling very insecure. So I put all the cash I had under our home, which I thought was a safe place. About one week later, I heard a rumor that the

IRS had taken drug dogs and searched through both stores looking for drugs. Of course, there weren't any drugs to be found. I always thought drugs were for weak people, and the IRS had ruled that scenario out in a week's time.

So, I got to thinking more and more about my circumstances with the money. I thought if the IRS could come in with armed men and forcefully take everything I owned, then why couldn't they come into my home and search my home? If they did a search, then they would take my cash, just like they took my stores. They had also seized ninety-four thousand dollars out of my company's bank account with no hearing or any accounting of what I did owe. So I figured they could come to my home, take the only money I had to fight them with, and therefore leave me totally helpless.

A few days later, I took my son Kenny to a location off of I-75 North at the Pate Road exit, about eight miles north of Macon. There was a large tract of land on the right of the exit ramp, and it is owned by the federal government. So Kenny and I went in the woods there on that exit ramp to locate a spot to hide the money I had.

I found an old large trunk of a tree, about two feet high, in the middle of the woods. I dug and hollowed it out. We then put all the cash in a mason jar, about eighty thousand dollars, all in one hundred dollar bills. I thought in plain sight is often the best way to hide anything. Why not on federal land. After all, they stole all my assets with no legal proceedings.

I placed a lot of bark and leaves over the jar to disguise it. It was all the money I had left in the world to fight the forces of evil, the IRS. I did not know if I would ever get my stores back because the IRS had told me that I could never return to my own business, thereby taking away my source for making a living. I buried the jar upside down so hopefully a metal detector could not detect it. I put all the leaves back in place and looked around a few minutes and left.

I told Grace that I had heard rumors of the IRS killing people like me in the north. She had thought that could be true mainly because they kept a car parked at the top of our driveway twenty-four hours a day, watching us for several weeks. She had also noticed a car following her everywhere she went every day, and she was terrified. I did not fear them, but I never drove anywhere close to my stores. They stole the stores from me, and I would not go back till God let me have them back through the courts. I think they were surprised that I never once went on that side of town. I am quite sure they followed me as well.

We were not sure what part of the US Government was doing this to us as an act of further intimidation. I guessed they thought we really had some serious money, but unfortunately we did not.

The next week, my son Kenny and my brother Harry got jobs working at Tom Stimus Chevrolet in Forsyth, just fifteen miles north of Macon, selling cars. This would take Kenny daily by the location where the money was hidden.

One cold, rainy night, Grace and I went to the dealership in Forsyth to see Kenny. Kenny came out in the pouring rain to see us. Grace started to cry like a baby, and tears began running out of my eyes after Kenny said, "Mama, I will be all right. Don't worry. I will be just fine!"

Here he was a six-foot-two, twenty-one-year-old man, and his wife, Melissa, had just found out that she was pregnant with my first grandchild three days prior to the assault seizure. Bravely, Kenny was standing there saying he was going to be okay.

When Kenny said he would be okay, it was then that all of this IRS mess hit me like a ton of bricks. I knew I had done a lot to hurt my family, and it made me feel horrible. I went from being a hero to a loser to my family overnight, putting shame on my whole family in middle Georgia.

Grace told Kenny, "Go back in, Son, before you get a cold. I love you."

I said, "I love you too, Son, very much!"

Kenny said, "I love you, Daddy. Everything will come out fine, Daddy, because you are a winner!"

I drove out thinking, Wow, my twenty-one-year-old son, Kenny, thinks I am still a winner. He has more faith in me than I do in myself right now.

I returned to the site where I stashed the money off of Pate Road exit about three months after hiding it there. I had to have some money to live on and pay attorney's fees. Fortunately, it was there, just as I left it, and I was very thankful.

Aftershock of the Seizure

As he had come naked from his mother's womb, so will he return as he came. He will take nothing from the fruit of his labor that he can carry in his hand.

Ecclesiastes 6:15

I was told by my accountant that I still had to come up with an answer as to where the one hundred thousand dollars came from that the IRS was questioning me about. The fact is one lie leads to another lie!

Grace and I first met with Bonnie Waldrep, the IRS civil auditor, in 1984 with Billy Lamb, my accountant, for a few minutes. Upon leaving, Grace told me that that IRS lady looked very familiar.

So I went to Daddy's wife, Toni, the woman he was married to after Mother passed away in 1966. Toni was twenty-five years younger than my daddy, and I had not seen her since Daddy passed in 1977. I asked her if she would tell the IRS that I got the money from

Daddy. That was a lie from me. I told her I would help her out with money if she would help me.

Jay Hawkins, my tax attorney, called for a hearing after the stores were closed for four weeks and asked me to go before Judge Duross Fitzpatrick in an effort to get my stores reopened. If I could get the stores reopened, then that would give me the opportunity to try and repay the alleged taxes that I owed the IRS.

Toni showed up at the hearing, to my surprise, and made a fool of me and told the court I had asked her to lie for me. I was justifying my lie in my mind because the forces of evil, the IRS and Bonnie Waldrep, had tricked me in 1985 from my attorney's office. The call from there undeniably broke my constitutional rights. It looked very bad on my part, and Jay then instructed me to never ever talk to Toni again for the rest of my life, and I agreed. To this day, I have never spoken to Toni again and never plan to. I was wrong doing that and paid a heavy price for trying to cover up my sin.

The stores had been closed for about four weeks, and it was just before Christmas time when we had the hearing. Judge Fitzpatrick asked the IRS agent Schwab at the hearing, "Who had authorized such drastic actions?"

Agent Schwab replied, "Someone in Washington."

Then Judge Fitzpatrick asked, "Who would that be?"

Agent Schwab replied, "I do not know." Again, this shows another pattern of deceit by the IRS Agent Schwab.

This man, Gary Schwab, started the criminal investigation in 1982 under the disguise of a civil case, and he still tells the federal judge that he does not know. The judge then asked, "How can Mr. Jones pay his taxes if he does not have his business open to do so?" Agent Schwab did not have a reply to that question, because it made common sense. I do not think these two words, common sense are in the IRS tax code of seventy thousand pages.

The IRS answers to no one and has the absolute power to destroy people's lives at will. The IRS is confident in their actions all the time, as they know they are unstoppable. This is one reason why we need to abolish the IRS, and have a Fair Tax tax system. I will address this issue later in the book.

So Judge Fitzpatrick ordered the stores to be reopened, and the IRS was furious. I walked out and asked them if I could get some money from the IRS that they had stolen from me to reopen the stores. When I posed that question to them, the IRS just laughed in my face and walked away.

With all of the publicity that we received from the activities involving the IRS, and with the obvious hatred that people have for the IRS, we had the best Christmas season ever! Praise God! I had a lot of folks during that time after the judge allowed me to reopen the stores that came in the store to see and tell me about their horror stories of abuse by the IRS. The IRS works on fear, which is of Satan.

In just four weeks, my home sold for 470,000 dollars. The IRS attended the closing and received approximately three hundred thousand dollars at the closing, and they were smiling and rubbing it in. Grace took the loss of our home a lot harder than I did. I felt deep inside it was wrong, since there was absolutely no proof of what I exactly owed to the IRS. But how could I fight the government when they had armed government men take my only way to make a living away by force? Here again, no hearing or proof of any taxes owed even then, and we were forced to move out before Christmas in 1986. I think this is why my case is in the Russian law books, because this action is like the communist way of law, in my belief, and how they treat their people.

Also, two days prior to Christmas the IRS auctioned my cars, and they bought in another $50,000 to them as I mentioned before. So within six weeks the IRS had already collected by force from me and my businesses almost a half-million dollars. All of this collection was done without any proof of what taxes I actually owed.

During this time, Mr. Casteel approached me and said that they had an offer from Hi-fi Buys in Atlanta to purchase my store in Macon. He said you can keep the store in Warner Robins, but we want to go ahead and secure the purchase of your Macon store with them. I looked at him in total disbelief and told him, "Mr. Casteel that is not going to happen, you will have to just go ahead and kill me because I am not going to sell the Macon store!" He just walked away and left.

I cashed in my life insurance policy and bought Grace a six-thousand-dollar, four-year-old, blue Cadillac. I was feeling very insecure and did not know what my attorney fees were going to be. I had also leased a home for nine hundred dollars a month in Devenwood off of

Forsyth Road in Macon for Grace, my eighteen-year-old son, Michael, and myself to live in.

I began to notice that Grace was acting very distant toward me, and I knew we had grown apart as a married couple. We had not had God in our lives for several years, plus we had not attended church in years. Grace seemed to be a person I did know anymore, plus the fact I had changed to be a person that I did not recognize anymore.

The daily stress was just awful between Grace and me, even though I was working again. I had no idea what events were next from the IRS. I had always assured Grace that I would protect her as I had of all our marriage. I told her that the IRS only wanted me. I would take all of the blame and punishment and full responsibility.

At end of April 1987, it happened. Grace just disappeared—vanished! I looked everywhere in Macon for her and also drove to all our friends' homes. I was totally devastated. I began to drink beer very heavily day and night. I often drove to Atlanta and back in the evenings, drinking beer, trying to drown my feelings of Grace being gone from my life. Grace had always been there in my times of need, and now she was gone, and it was driving me crazy. The one person I needed was now gone, even though I knew deep inside the love was not there between us that we once shared. Losing material things I could handle, but losing people in my life took the very personal part of my life apart. I had always had Grace by my side basically all my adult life as a friend and a sounding board. I was one lost soul.

Her disappearance went on for a month. Then one day God gave me a feeling that I should stay at home, and I did. I parked my car up the street away from my home and walked back to my home. I was sitting in the living room for a few hours, and in walked Grace with four Bibb County deputy sheriffs. I asked her, "Where have you been, and why do you have the sheriff's deputies with you?"

One of the deputies replied, "We are here to protect her."

I was stunned and hurt deep inside. I asked Grace, "What have you told them? Have I ever hurt you in our twenty-three years of marriage?"

Grace replied no, and the deputies just looked at her in awe.

I asked the four deputies to wait outside so I could talk to my wife for ten minutes and I would not do anything stupid. I told them, "You guys know me." They respected me and walked outside to allow us a private moment.

I looked at Grace, and I told her that I was concerned about her. The first thing she said was, "I want a divorce." I told her that I understood. I told her that I needed her now more than ever, and she replied that she was doing me a favor. I told Grace that I did not do anything close to what the IRS was saying and she knew that as a fact. Grace told me that I could not win this time, and she further stated, "I just want a divorce!"

Grace told me that we were both miserable, and she was right on both issues. I told her I would do the right thing by her, and with that she asked for half of the money we had, which was thirty thousand in cash at that time. I told her I would give the money to her when she signed over the stores and signed the divorce papers. I told her I would give the fifteen thousand dollars to Kenny the day the divorce was final. I told her she could have all of the furniture, et cetera, and I would pay her money for three years out of my rent money, since I would most likely be going to prison. I told Grace that I wished her only the best and would pay for all of her legal bills.

That was it. In about ten minutes, twenty-three years of my married life was down the drain. I told the sheriff's deputies to come back in, and they helped her load her clothes. I just left and told her I would not be there when she returned to get the furniture and the balance of her clothes.

Strange as it seems, I thought that when you get a divorce it seems like it is just someone you used to know; when it's over, it's over. How wrong I was!

I thought it was over when Grace moved out, but deep depression set in, and I was drinking more because I was confused and lost. Michael, now eighteen, had moved out to an apartment of his own.

One evening at about 7:00 p.m., the IRS criminal investigator Gary Schwab came knocking on my door at my home in July 1987. Mr. Schwab knew this was an illegal act because my attorney was not present, and he also knew that my divorce was final. He knew that I would be in a weakened state of mind. The IRS has absolute power, and they consider themselves to be above the law.

He asked me if Michael was paying me any rent, like twenty dollars a week. I told him of course not. He got mad and left. I found out in 1989 that there is a law that states if I had another source of income, no matter how small—even twenty dollars a week—that the IRS could have sold my stores and everything I had.

This is just one of the many ways I can attest to about how unscrupulous the IRS was then and how corrupt they are. God had his hand on me, and Schwab did not know that, even in my weakest time.

I started looking for a home to buy even with the liens on me. I found a home on Lake Tobesofkee that a friend of mine owned, and I was able to assume his loan. My credit was never tarnished.

The pain for Grace in my heart would not go away. I was just killing myself with grief and loneliness, and it felt as though part of me had died. We had been best friends and gone from being dirt poor to rich, raised two fine sons, and then back to poor with the full weight of the government on my back. But, I still had hope that someday this would be over and that I would survive this battle.

Grace wanted to distance herself from me, and I understood that. She also told me that I would never win this battle. I was wrong, and I admitted my sins to God, and the IRS already knew everything through trickery and deception.

I could not find peace within myself. I was lost from within.

The hole in my heart was just getting bigger even though we were divorced. I thought I was a very strong man, but I just could not shake this feeling I had. So, I did what I always had done when things were too big for me to handle. I just turned it over to Jesus. One afternoon, I did something I had never done before in my life.

I went into my bedroom closet and dropped to my knees and started to pray and pray fervently for quite some time. I prayed for Jesus to take Grace out of my heart and mind, in the name of Jesus, over and over. I prayed for a long while, and all of a sudden the Holy Spirit came over me—a cleansing feeling unlike I had ever experienced before.

The power of Jesus was just awesome! I actually felt the great burden of my relationship with Grace lifted off my shoulders, and she was gone out of my heart and mind.

I got off my knees, and I was soaking wet from head to toe without even knowing what or how long I had been praying. I felt like a new man, pure from within. The feeling was so awesome. I walked around the house just praising Jesus out loud, over and over. I was now free to go on with my life against the forces of evil, the IRS. There is truly victory in Jesus and his healing powers!

The power of prayer had saved me again!

My mind was clear for the fight of my life!

About two months later, my phone rang one Sunday night about 10:30pm, in late August, 1987. When I answered the phone there was the voice of a woman whom I did not recognize. I asked, "Who is this?" And she answered, "Grace!" She said she had been ironing clothes and just wanted to call and see how I was doing. I told her I was so sorry not to have recognized her voice but that God had lifted the burden of her off of me that I was carrying and that she was no longer in my heart. I told her I wished her only the best and hung up the phone. I knew then that God had truly answered my prayer because I no longer missed her.

I found out that God loves you because of who God is, not because of anything you did or didn't do!

> Now what will you do on the day of punishment. And in the day of devastation which will come from afar? To whom will you flee for help? And where will you leave your wealth?
>
> Isaiah 10:3

Day of Reckoning

The Bible is very clear on this subject, for sure, "Your sins will find you out."

> But if ye will not do so, behold, you have sinned against the Lord: and be sure your sins will find you out.
>
> Numbers 32:23

Even though I was tricked and deceived by the IRS, for four years from day one in 1982, I had done wrong. It did not make a difference. You will see the many laws that the IRS horrifically broke. When the IRS takes aim at an American citizen for one reason, they think the end justifies the means. The IRS knows they have absolute power. They have the full resources of the government at their disposal.

The IRS knows they have absolute power to place liens on anyone, anytime, and you are assumed guilty from the beginning.

So months rocked on, and in 1988 it was a new year, and my criminal attorney was telling me how we were going to fight all the wrongdoings that the IRS had been doing to me. He said also for what they had already done to me. So I went to another high-profile attorney in Atlanta and asked him where I stood. I told him everything.

The new attorney told me that I would get three years prison time because the IRS was all about the money. If the dollar amounts were between two hundred fifty thousand and one million dollars, as the IRS was purporting, then that would be the amount of time for my sentence. He also told me that the judge always believed the IRS. I told him the amount they were quoting was incorrect. He told me that did not matter because the IRS can lie all they want. "Your civil trial has not happened yet to prove what is the correct amount you owe, so you have nothing to back up your case."

I finally got the stores financially stable and was paying the bills about forty-five to sixty days past due. The IRS had made it really tough by collecting 5 percent of all the gross sales. The IRS figured that would break me eventually.

I was over Grace, and she was right, she did me a favor by leaving me. I had stopped drinking beer all the time and was really concentrating on earning money for the stores. It was extremely hard to start over with no capital, since the IRS had taken the ninety-four thousand dollars in October 1986 from the stores. Those funds were in our operating funds account.

I had gone by the office of my accountant, Mr. Freeman, and he had just gotten back from a CPA convention in Savannah, Georgia. Mr. Freeman said he had heard an amazing speaker from Atlanta there that he thought could help me. He said the speaker's name was David Aughtry and gave me his phone number. At that moment, I was very depressed and was down to driving a $6,000 Mercury Marquee with a ragged out top with eighty-four thousand miles on it. I had one of the first large cell phones with me, and I had great hesitation in calling him because I was out of money and would be unable to pay him a retainer. But I got to thinking about what I had promised Kenny, "Win I would, if the IRS did not kill me, so help me God," so I picked up the phone and called David Aughtry in Atlanta.

I got through to David and starting telling him all about my IRS mess and he stopped me in my tracks and told me, "You must come up to my office first thing in the morning." The next morning I was at his office at Peachtree Street in Atlanta at nine a.m. David was totally amazed about everything I was telling him about what the IRS had done to me. I told him that I was broke but if he could help me that I would pay him the best I could. By the grace of God, he accepted my case, and I gave him Jay Hawkins's number in Macon, because he was my local tax attorney in Macon that knew everything about my case.

Walking out of his office, I felt as though it was not an accident that my accountant had gone to Savannah and heard David and told me about him. I did not know what, when, or how, but I knew that God was definitely working in my life. I knew that God was doing something very good for me in regards to the help I could get from David Aughtry, and at that moment I started thanking God for his help. I realized like the song that I love so much, that the God on the mountain is the same God in the valley. Praise to God that he allowed me to meet David. It was now David verses Goliath (the IRS).

I was paying attorney fees, and working six days a week and then bam!—it happened—my criminal indictment in April 1988. Eighteen months had passed since the assault by the IRS. This was another example of my constitutional rights being broken; in fact it is the Sixth Amendment that you are supposed to be granted a speedy trial? It was one year and six months? And the fact remains that I was never read my Miranda Rights.

My Criminal attorney, Jay Hawkins, my tax attorney, and I met in Jay's library at his office.

Looking me in the eyes, my criminal attorney said, "Ken, you have never gotten into trouble for anything, and narcotics were not involved. This is your first offense, plus you are a model citizen." I do not believe you will get any more than four months' time in prison. I responded and told him that I had talked to another attorney and he told me that I would get three years and that I do not think the stores will survive three years.

My criminal attorney told me that the IRS would drop all other charges if I would plead guilty to two counts of filing false income tax returns for 1981 and 1983. I reluctantly agreed but I felt deep inside my constitutional rights had been broken by the IRS.

My Day in Court, What a Day!

All of the IRS agents were there from Macon and Atlanta in the Macon courthouse. Also attending the plea and sentencing were my son Kenny, my daughter-in-law Melissa, and the press. Outside the courthouse I was told that there were several local TV stations, like I was Al Capone!

Judge Duross Fitzpatrick had just been appointed a federal judge by President Ronald Reagan, and I was his first tax case. There were guidelines for sentencing that had started in the early eighties.

The judge asked me to stand up and then asked me if I understood the charges and the consequences and if I was of sound mind. He also asked if I was promised anything, and to this I replied no.

Judge Fitzpatrick stated, "You have been a model citizen, and you have done a lot of good deeds for middle Georgia, but you, Mr. Jones, are the victim of man's oldest sin: greed!" And I did not say a word. (How wrong he was!) He continued by saying, "Mr. Jones, I sentence you to three years under the jurisdiction of the United States Attorney General. Also, you will have five years' probation and a twenty-five thousand dollar fine, plus payment of all back-taxes owed to the government." The judge then slammed down the hammer and ran out of the courtroom.

The joy that was on the faces of the IRS agents was very evident. They were all smiling broadly. They had finally completely destroyed Ken Jones (they thought) on something they had started six years earlier in 1982.

I remained calm. I was not in tears as the paper later stated. This statement I believe came from the IRS people.

I turned around and looked at Schwab and he was grinning and I just smiled at him in return and he looked surprised. I smiled at him because he did not have a clue that he was dealing with a man that would never ever quit.

Since I was a well know business man, the judge gave me two months to get my business in order before having to report to prison. I did not have to post bail, so I was on my own recognizance. They did a background check on me and then determined that I would be able to serve my prison time in a minimum-security-type prison—Maxwell Air Force Base Work Prison Camp in Montgomery, Alabama.

As a family, we walked outside of the courthouse together. The TV crews were set up so I would be on the news that night, and the IRS people were very happy. My youngest son, Michael, bless his soul, was only nineteen and very scared and just sat in his car during the court proceedings. That day was a blur in my mind!

On the way back to the store, a news bulletin came on all of the radio stations by the IRS. It was on the radio stations within fifteen minutes of the sentencing. The IRS has great power to destroy a person in the media. I heard, "Ken Jones, of Ken's Stereo Junction, got three years for income tax evasion!" I had hit the big time now! I could not believe it was already being broadcast so quickly.

I had humiliated my family for eighteen months, and now I had made the news again. I was going to prison for three years, and it was on TV, on the radio, and in the newspapers.

The IRS did a great job breaking all of my constitutional rights for six years and branding me as a bad man. The IRS seized all of my assets with U.S. Marshals pulling pistols on me in my own business, and my wife of twenty-three years divorces me, and now I am sentenced to go to prison for three years! All of this happened in eighteen months.

I told my son Kenny, now twenty-three, "Win I will, if the IRS does not kill me, so help me God!"

One thing the IRS did not count on was the fact that I had Jesus in my heart, and thereby God on my side, plus the gift of a visionary mind! I knew deep down inside I was in this position for a reason, and I did not know why. But I had done wrong and was going to take my punishment as a man and blame no one but myself.

I vowed never to give up on hope and my faith in Jesus Christ, for he had forgiven me! The only good hope in the world is based on Jesus Christ, my Lord and Savior, and I would not be denied that!

It did not matter how many lies or acts of perjury against me that the IRS agents, Bonnie Waldrep or Gary Schwab, told on me, for I knew the truth would prevail!

The secret of winning is never quitting—this was a saying I created during my seven-year battle with the forces of evil, the IRS!

Instruct those who are rich in this present world not to be conceited or not to fix their hope on the uncertainty of riches, but on God, but to put their hope in God, who richly supplies us with all things to enjoy.

1 Timothy 6:17

Macon stereo store owner gets 3-year jail term for tax evasion

By Tom Carroll
Macon Telegraph and News

A federal judge sentenced the owner of Ken's Stereo Junction stores in Macon and Warner Robins Thursday to three years in prison for two counts of income tax evasion.

U.S. District Court Judge Duross Fitzpatrick sentenced Kenneth Jones for failure to pay about $340,000 in taxes in 1981 and 1983.

Under a plea bargain arranged by defense attorneys and prosecutors in April, charges of filing a false income tax return in 1982, obstruction of justice and criminal fraud were dropped.

Fitzpatrick had little sympathy for the sobbing Jones as he explained the rationale for his decision.

"Mr. Jones is a victim of one of the oldest afflictions of mankind — greed," he said.

"This country depends on the voluntary payment of taxes," he added. Taxpayers must decide "to buy a new house, buy a new car, or send a child to college (based) on how much is left after taxes," Fitzpatrick said.

Jones didn't need the withheld tax money for family necessities but to "maintain a certain lifestyle," Fitzpatrick said.

Fitzpatrick said that Jones let his obsession with material wealth overcome him.

"Unfortunately, it came in the form of tax evasion," he said.

Defense attorney Frank Childs said that Jones had suffered enough from the trauma of the ordeal. He said that the investigation and ensuing publicity had cost Jones his marriage, hundreds of thousands of dollars, and three years of "embarrassment and humiliation."

Childs reasoned that Jones should not be incarcerated because he had suffered enough and he was a threat to nobody.

Jones has paid approximately $742,000 in back taxes, but he still owes about $1 million in taxes, penalties and interest, Assistant U.S. Attorney Miriam Duke said. Jones will be on probation for five years following his

(See JONES, page 2B)

Prison Life

For all have sinned, and fall short of the glory
of God.

Romans 3:23

I was ordered to report on June 27, 1988, to Maxwell
Air Force Base Work Prison Camp in Montgomery,
Alabama. My son Kenny was twenty-three years old,
and my brother Harry was thirty-two when they drove
me what seemed like a very long way from Macon
to Montgomery, Alabama. The trip took about three
hours, and it was a hard drive, no interstates and all
small two-lane roads. The drive was very arduous
because I was so very apprehensive about all of it. I
also did not know how they were going to treat me at
the prison.

Maxwell Work Camp is a minimum-security work
camp, but I was unsure of what I had to face. I had
spoken to a man who had been there years prior for
some kind of fraud. He told me that listing all of my
ailments would help me later on down the line as to

what they would assign for my work detail. He told me that it would be helpful also because I was a business owner. He said that guys like me usually got office jobs. I would turn forty-four in prison that following July.

In June of 1988, my assets were depleted down to an old maroon 1984 Mercury that I had purchased in 1987 for six thousand dollars. The car had a ragged-out top with about eighty-five thousand miles on it. I gave my son Kenny what cash I had left to keep at his home till I got out of prison.

One of my relatives purchased the car from me for five thousand dollars, because I obviously did not need a car. My money was very tight since the IRS was taking 5 percent of the gross sales. I believe the IRS's hope was that the stores would lose enough money and that the business would close while I was in prison.

My brother Harry was in charge of the stores, bless his soul, but he was the baby in our family and not a take-charge type of person like I was. My son Kenny was too young to run the stores, and my other son, Michael, was only nineteen years old at the time. The IRS knew I was a helpless person in prison. When we arrived at Maxwell AFB to go through to the back of the air force base, I noticed it was very clean and maintained.

Getting out of the car at the prison, I noticed there were no fences, and I saw people walking around in green clothes. I turned around to wave good-bye to my son Kenny and my brother Harry as they drove off. I had only my bag of clothes in my hand. I felt very lonesome as they drove away and left me to my new way of life in prison.

I walked into the office and was greeted by a very obese young lady that looked to be about thirty years old. I told her who I was and handed her my papers. She started barking orders to me real rudely.

A little later, about four more new inmates in orange jumpsuits walked over by the building waiting on further instructions. We did not know any better, so the four of us started talking to each other.

I talked to one guy named Joey Justice. Joey was the former president of five banks in Florida. Joey also told me that he was a former bank president at a C&S Bank in Macon, Georgia, in 1984. I remembered hearing his name, and he remembered Ken's Stereo Junction. There was also another guy named Tom Sawyer, who was a pilot with Eastern Airlines. Tom admitted that he got caught flying marijuana in on a flight from Columbia, and he had gotten five years of prison time for that. He was big and strong—very muscular, kind of like Sean Connery, good looking guy, but arrogant, talking as though he knew it all.

Meanwhile, the hack (a hack is what inmates call a prison guard) walked over to us and said, "Come on, guys, we are going to go to work." So we walked over to where they were building three new dormitories at that time. They were tearing down the old dormitories from the twenties.

Those dormitories had been where Charles Colson and John Mitchell had been from the Watergate days in the mid-seventies. The old dormitories were actually built for the army in World War I, and they were making room for the new ones. I was fortunate enough to serve my time at the new dormitories. The three new dormitories were two stories high and were named after the cities in Alabama, such as Mobile, Dothan, and Birmingham. I was located in the Mobile section C.

One thing I noticed when they took me to the building where I would be living that was really odd, the brick that was used was the same brick color and pattern as the home I had built in Macon, Woodcrest Manor. I thought to myself, How ironic; well here I am going from one big house to another really "big house."

The first weekend, being brand-new inmates, we all three got kitchen duty. Joey and Tom were obviously smarter than I was. Tom got in the front of the line to put the dishes in and Joey put the dishes in the dishwasher and I got the duty of picking up the hot dishes. The gloves were filthy, so I would not put them on, and the dishes were just too hot to hold and stack.

This was just like the old I Love Lucy sitcom with the cakes rolling off the line in the fifties; I just could not keep up with the hot dishes. So the dishes began to crash all over in the floor while Tom and Joey were laughing their heads off. I was the dummy at the end of the dish detail, and they set me up for being stupid. This went on for ten minutes, and I guess about one hundred dishes were broken before a hack came back there and saw the mess. He shut down the dishwasher and asked what my name was then fired me. Looking back, it is sort of funny now! I had been in prison just three days and was fired already!

I did make a really big mistake. While I was in the kitchen that day, I saw a very tall black male smoking in there. There were no-smoking laws even in the eighties on all military bases. But one thing I did not know was to never ever tell on another inmate. After I told a hack about this black man smoking in the kitchen, the hack got him. As he walked by me, the inmate gave me a very bad feeling. His look was very evil, like Satan, and he stared at me like that all the way walking out.

The very next day I saw this same tall black inmate doing a karate workout with his legs and arms behind a building with two other men as lookouts. It was illegal for him to do this deadly art in prison, from what I had been told. I had never seen a man move as fast as he did. He looked at me with that same evil look. It reminded me of how my daddy looked at me when I was a little boy.

The next day, I asked another black man about this man, and he said he was in there for allegedly killing an FBI agent with his hands, but they could not prove it. That afternoon, one of the black man's friends told me that he was going to kill me, and I had only been in prison six days! So that afternoon I went to my bunk and prayed. I knew I did not have chance of defending myself against this man. Just one blow from him to my neck would kill me.

As always, I went to a power much bigger than me. I just prayed to be in God's will, and that was it. I was in prison of my own doing. I was going to be a man no matter what, and I truly was a "child of the King."

To my surprise, the very next morning I saw a busload of new inmates come in the camp and saw five inmates get on the bus from the Maxwell AFB Prison

Camp. As I was observing this, I realized something wonderful; I saw that my prayer had been answered!

The black karate man that was threatening to kill me was getting on the bus to go to another prison. I asked another inmate why he was being moved, and he told me that he was here by mistake. His sentence was for fifteen years, and the minimum security camps are for inmates with five years or less. Praise God, my prayers were answered because that was a really close call!

The food at the prison was absolutely terrible. I ate very little of the food, because it was so awful. The meat was very questionable as to what it was. I ate just a little of the food, because it did not have any taste. I mostly ate salad every night. When you are depressed you eat very little anyway and sleep a lot. I found out that this was the case for all new inmates including myself. I lost thirty pounds in two months.

At that time, I was kind of in limbo, and they told me I was going to be in section Mobile, section C. I went into that area, and I got the top bunk. Since I was a new guy, being on top bunk, the overhead light was only about eighteen inches above my head. This of course made the light directly in my face. So, I dealt with the light until about 10:00 p.m. At about 9:00 p.m. they would do a headcount so we would have to stand by our bed, like we were in the army, for them to do the count.

I found out they did the headcount to make sure that no one had left the camp. Because it was an open minimum security, you could walk out if you dared. At 10:00 p.m., they did "lights out," and we went to bed.

At 6:00 a.m. they turned on all the lights, and then we walked to breakfast at the camp.

The next day I listed my skills, and they found out that I knew how to answer the phone, type, and how to do office work, since I had owned a business. They assigned me to the psychiatrist's office in the camp. I went to work in her office, and she was really rude to me, and it was terribly boring. She would talk down to me all the time. I worked as the receptionist for her office, but I had the privilege of a small radio that I could listen to.

While in this office I was feeling very depressed listening to the little radio, and a song I heard gave me hope. The song was just what I needed at that moment. It was by the Four Seasons, a group I used to listen to in high school, "Walk Like a Man." I spoke a prayer and said, I must do this and "Walk Like a Man!" I felt so much better after a few moments that God lifted me up! There is great power in prayer! I was used to communicating, and just sitting around made me bored out of my mind. I became very depressed.

I found out the federal government has a fear of lawsuits against them. The government has three big weaknesses and they are race, religion, and health. They do not want those types of lawsuits against them. The government has to pay for your healthcare, as well, while you are in prison.

The feds don't want you to be able to file a lawsuit of any type. As an inmate, you do have rights even as an American citizen. The IRS treated me as though I had no rights for four years prior to the assault in 1986; this you will see was tried and proved in 1989! I actually had a lot more rights in prison than I experienced with the IRS during all of this time.

My back was bothering me from sitting there all day at the desk. I told the psychiatrist that my back was bothering me a lot and I wanted to file for another job. She replied, "You can't do that!"

I said, "Yes, ma'am, I am going to do that or file a lawsuit." I went ahead and filed my papers to be moved out of that office.

I remembered one time somebody laid some papers by the door while she was at lunch. Upon her return she yelled at me to pick up the papers. I had all I could take from her. She said, "Pick those papers up!" as if I was less than a human being to her.

I said, "I am a person, just like you are, and I have feelings, just like you have, and I am not a slave; I am a child of the King! I am not picking up those papers, have you got that?" She looked at me and she backed down when I told her that.

She knew I was talking about Jesus Christ, and she looked at me and did not say another word. She picked up the papers, and she asked me to leave. So I left and never looked back. I think it was the fear of a religious lawsuit!

My chief hack was the captain. The captain said, "Well, Jones, what is the matter?"

I said, "My back is bothering me big time and hurting from sitting there all day, and I want to be moved."

"Well we will put you on grass detail."

"No, if you will look at my medical records, I can't do that much walking because my ankles swell up."

"Well, Jones, what can you do?"

"I can do a lot of things."

"Well," he said, "we can do one thing; we can put you on outbound assignments. That is where you be on the move a lot and you won't be sitting down very much. Since you owned a business, I know you can type and you can talk."

"Yes sir!" I said.

He said, "Okay, we are going to put you on outbound assignments with four sergeants and a captain outside the camp on the air force base. You will ride the bus back and forth to your work assignments.

Being assigned to outbound assignment was a blessing, and they allowed me to work there my entire time at the camp. I reported to the captain and got along great with the air force people. They were all very kind to me.

Believe it or not, the air force people treated the inmates like pets. They asked me what I was in there for, and I told them the truth and we all became friends. The Maxwell air force folks treated us like real people. The inmates always got all the leftovers after the parties they had when an officer was being transferred. I felt like a human being on the base.

The air force personnel called us by our first names, and I immediately found out what my job entailed. I had to pick up records at the hospital and several other places. I also picked up the records for people being shipped around the world, even to Warner Robins

Air Force Base, which is thirty miles south of Macon, Georgia. It would always make my heart swell up and make me teary eyed. I missed my family so much.

The captain even wrote a letter to Judge Duross Fitzpatrick. The letter told him I had been doing a great job for them and had been a good man for the five months I had been serving there.

Judge Fitzpatrick wrote me back and said, "Dear Mr. Jones, Thank you for your letter that you are getting along so well in your job in there, for you are going to be there a long time, Sincerely, Judge Duross Fitzpatrick."

I had to laugh when I got the letter because it showed that he had a good sense of humor. The judge did not have to answer, because being a federal judge is right up there in power next to the president. I really respected Judge Fitzpatrick for being so kind to even respond to me, for he was a very good Christian man.

Meanwhile, my sons were coming to see me every weekend, and we spent eight to ten hours with each other. It was unbelievable how you can spend that much time together and how fast it went by. We had an outside place where we could meet in an auditorium.

This outside area was where in the Watergate days there was a swimming pool, and Barbara Walters made it famous by interviewing Charles Colson there in 1976. There was such a public outcry about the swimming pool that the government filled in the pool and publicly nicknamed the prison Club Fed.

It was now a sitting area for inmates since the prison population had grown from two hundred to nine hundred inmates from the seventies to my time in

1988. There is a resort in France by the name of Club Med, hence the name Club Fed. Believe me, this was no resort!

My sons and I would talk about the different inmates there and what they were in there for. We would talk about everything, and we really bonded for life at that point forever. It was very hard for me when they left to go home. I would often stand outside and watch them drive away with tears in my eyes.

I had other friends come visit and my brother Harry.

Meanwhile, I got used to being in prison and made a lot of friends of my own kind. There were bankers, doctors, one judge, three sheriffs from Georgia, and other businessmen, all in there with me while I was serving my time.

Two times a week an older movie was shown. On Tuesday nights I would go to church that was a Pentecostal church meeting. The people would come from a local church and the elder preacher would bring his wife and his sister. He was a really good man of God, and it made me feel at home to go to an Assembly of God Pentecostal meeting there at Maxwell Air Force Base. It was a small room, with only room for about thirty people, and about that many would come to every church meeting. I would take my Bible, and we would have singing, and the minister would preach. Attending the church service meeting would make me feel very good, and I actually forgot I was in prison. I looked forward to every Tuesday night church meeting.

I read the entire Bible through twice while I was in prison. I had never taken time to read the Bible like that before, because I always considered myself too busy.

I remember one day a young black man in his twenties came to me and asked me if I could read, and I replied, "Yes."

He said, "Sir, would you read my mama's letter to me?"

I said, "Of course." I read the three-page letter to the young man, and tears started to flow down his cheeks. He was wiping the tears away, and I said, "It is okay, you will be fine." He just smiled and walked away saying thank you. So every time he got a letter from his mama, he came to me, and I read the letters to him. I never knew his name, but I felt blessed to be able to help him in his time of need. I often wondered why he picked me out of nine hundred men!

The Lord was not in my life those years while I was working to make the almighty dollar, and that was one of my biggest failures: leaving God out of my life! Money was my God then during those years, and I never thought about how I had left God out of my life!

In thinking back about that time in prison, I made a lot of friends there, and people actually liked me as a person. I was not the same Kenneth Jones in there that I had been on the outside. My personality had changed completely while I was in there, and I got into a daily routine. God had taken the arrogance away from me and humbled me.

I also found out an awful lot about people too; one thing I noticed that people of like-kind stayed together. In that respect in the camp the Puerto Ricans stayed together, the Cubans stayed together, the African Americans stayed together, and the Jews stayed together. There were only nine Jews in there, in fact one was the nephew of Phil Spector, who was a famous producer. Also, there was a former governor of Tennessee in there prior to me. Also John Mitchell and Chuck Colson had served their time there for their Watergate days. Mitchell and Colson's time frame was back in the seventies when they had the old barracks.

One evening while walking around the camp, I noticed a very distinguished man with expensive eyeglasses just walking in the dark by the cafeteria crying. I walked up and said to him, "This is not the end of the world."

As he wiped away his tears, I introduced myself, and he said, "I am Ron Blackwood of the Blackwood Brothers Quartet." Since I was raised in the Pentecostal church, I was familiar with the quartet and knew they were famous in the world of gospel music.

Ron was very depressed, and I tried to encourage him. We quickly became friends because we both knew the Lord. Ron told me that he had lost everything—his twenty-eight-year-old wife and baby, his new three-hundred-thousand-dollar tour bus—and now he had prison time to deal with. I told him the first three months were the hardest to adjust to losing your freedom and your own free will. But I told him that he could overcome it all with prayer.

For whatever reason, Ron was also assigned to do outbound assignments as I was doing. Ron had an office about fifty feet from mine on the base. I really liked Ron, but he was breaking the rules by talking on the phone on the base. His sergeant liked Ron and let him call his mother. Ron even did a live talk show on a.m. radio after lunchtime in Montgomery from the prison on the phone! I told Ron, "You will get caught and reap what you sow!"

I tried to tell him that when he got caught he would be transferred to a real lockdown prison. Ron would not listen to me. About four months later, the hacks came and put him in handcuffs and put him in the hole (solitary confinement). The sergeant got demoted for letting him talk on the phone; but I guess someone on the base heard him on the radio.

Ron's uncle was the famous James Blackwood.

Getting caught on the phone cost Ron a lot. Ron was put in the hole. In the world of prisons, the hole is an eight-by-eight prison cell with only books to read, no TV. You are there for twenty-three hours of the day and are only allowed to walk by yourself in a fenced area for one hour per day. You are also only allowed one bath per week.

One night I was walking to the Pentecostal service that we had every Tuesday evening, and I heard Ron call out to me from the hole, "Ken, Ken, I need to talk to you!"

As I was walking I said, "I cannot talk to you," and ignored him and continued on my way.

I hated to do that to my friend, but the rule is if you get caught talking to an inmate in the hole, you will be put there also. That was the last time I saw Ron, and that has been fifteen plus years. I talked to him about four years ago by chance, and he said he was singing again and that his gospel group was performing in Gatlinburg, Tennessee, and in Branson, Missouri.

> But the Spirit explicitly says that in the latter times some will fall away from the faith, paying attention to deceitful spirits, and doctrines of demons.
>
> 1 Timothy 4:1

When Easter time rolled around, I had some friends who were Christians who wanted me to meet them at sunrise by the Alabama River to celebrate Easter. One of them was a former preacher and also a stockbroker from Marietta, Georgia, who gathered us together. We were there before sunrise, and it was just beautiful, for I felt the spirit of the Lord as if I was at home. I looked around, and out of nine hundred men, I counted the same number of men as the last supper—thirteen!

Yes, thirteen men were there to celebrate the fact that Christ has risen! Thank God that was the only Easter I had to be at that place.

As I had mentioned earlier in 1964, when I was a new Atlanta policeman, and it was there in 1989 that I noticed a black man who looked very familiar to me mainly because of his freckles and smile.

Now twenty-five years later, I saw the same man that looked like the young man from that time era. I saw several black inmates that were hanging around this man as though he was a celebrity, and I later realized who he was.

It is none other than former Atlanta police chief A. Reginald Eaves that served under Mayor Maynard Jackson between the years 1974 to 1978! He was forced to resign for some police scandal. The rumor was the FBI set up a sting operation where he took some $30,000 in cash in 1987 because at that time he was on the Fulton County Commissioners Board. He was then tried and sentenced to Maxwell AFB Federal Work Prison Camp as a result.

Thank God he got another chance like me!

I did one really stupid thing while in prison that could have cost me a lot more time in prison. I had a visitor come see me one weekend who bought me a six pack of beer for me and two of my inmate friends. They left it in an area at the base where I could retrieve it near the building where I worked.

Ah, I think now it was a lot like in the movie The Shawshank Redemption. I thought it tasted so good and made me feel like a man again. Or maybe it was the fact that I was doing something against the rules.

Unfortunately, not thinking very clearly, we stood over by a wall of the building and drank all of the beer in about ten minutes. Obviously, someone saw this and called the prison and reported to them that some of the inmates were on the base drinking beer. I knew somebody had snitched on us because when we all got on the buses to go back to the camp all of the inmates were being given alcohol tests. This had never happened, and I knew I was in big trouble! There were approximately seventy-five inmates in front of me to be tested, as the buses were unloading.

I immediately started praying fervently and telling God if he would get me out of this, that I would never, ever do this again! I just knew that I was bound for a maximum-security prison, because I knew I would test positive!

I was still making God promises and begging him to help me!

The captain came over to the line with about seventy-five guys waiting, and pointed at me and said, "You, you can go to your bunk!" I could not believe it, out of all of those guys, he picked only me not to be tested! I walked away thanking God quietly in my mind. I never again drank while in prison, because I had promised God, and he had definitely delivered me, again!

> ...yet with respect to the promise of God, he did not waver in unbelief but grew strong in faith, giving glory to God.
>
> Romans 4:20

Daddy's Prophecy

> And so we have the prophetic word made surer
> to which you do well to pay attention, as to
> a lamp shining in a dark place, until the day
> dawns, and the morning star arises in your
> hearts
>
> 2 Peter 1:19

One night I was in a deep sleep in my bed at Maxwell, when I woke up startled at 3:00 a.m. I suddenly remembered something very strange that had happened to me years before. My daddy's prophecy had been fulfilled!

While I was still working for Gulf Life as a district manager in August of 1977, my secretary, Suzanne, came in and told me that my daddy was on the phone, and she thought he was crying! My first thought was that it could not be, not my daddy. I had never seen him shed a tear. He had moved to Macon four years earlier to be close to me, and I had nothing to do with him for the most part. I guessed he was lonely and that was why he moved there.

Suzanne said Daddy had asked me to come to the Medical Center of Central Georgia because there was something very important he needed to tell me. I left and went to the hospital, and I was unaware at that time that he had experienced a second severe heart attack and had actually died but had been revived.

When I got there to see him, he told me that he had gone through an afterlife experience. Daddy told me that he had seen a bright light, and the light was so brilliant it burned his eyes. He also said he went through a tunnel, and the love of the Lord and the peace he felt were awesome. He told me that he did not want to come back.

Daddy's feelings were enormous and assured him that God loved him. He knew that God would accept him into heaven. But he was turned away because God had something he wanted me to know about a future event in my life.

Daddy begged me for forgiveness for the abuse he had given to me as a child. He also said that God wanted to warn me that something really, really, really bad was going to happen to me.

He said, "Kenneth, you are going to lose everything you had ever worked for all of your life. God said it will almost kill you, and Grace will leave you, too."

I asked Daddy, "What are you talking about?" Daddy then repeated verbatim everything he had just told me. I looked him straight in the eyes and said, "Why me? I do not understand. "What are you talking about?"

He replied that he did not know what it would be, but he continued and said, "It will almost kill you, but you will survive, and you will win! "Do you know why, Kenneth? You are a real man, and you know God. Because of the way I mistreated you as a child you will survive and win!"

Daddy told me that someday, after he was dead and gone, "You will remember this day and what I told you and what God told me to tell you!"

Daddy later told the same story to me to my other siblings and Daddy talked about this afterlife experience and the shining light over and over. He stated that he could not wait to go back to heaven to be with God. Almost three months later, on November 7, 1977, Daddy passed away and was granted his peace to go to heaven. Daddy's death was seven months prior to me opening Ken's Stereo Junction.

Of course, I had forgotten all about Daddy's afterlife experience until I woke up in my prison bed that night. God brought it vividly back to my memory at 3:00 a.m. that morning. This was eleven years after Daddy passed away!

I realized right then and there that everything Daddy had told me had come to pass. I knew that God had warned me through him. I embraced and held on to the assurance that I would survive this ordeal. I knew that everything was happening for a reason, even if I did not understand the reasons. I would survive it all!

I paid for daddy's tombstone as I had promised him before he died. He is buried outside of Leslie, Georgia, next to his grandmother. This was the grandmother who raised him and that he loved so much and died when he was eight years old. One thing he recalled about her was that she read the Bible every night to him. I put on his tombstone what he had talked about the last three months of his life: "The shining light at last!"

This vision came from God and was delivered to me miraculously through the Holy Spirit being channeled through my daddy. This undoubtedly should debunk all of the atheists' theories of there not being a true and living God!

> For no prophecy was ever made by an act of human will, but men moved by the Holy Spirit spoke from God.
>
> Peter 1:21

IRS Corruption Exposed

Do not judge lest you be judged.

Matthew 7:1

It had been three years and three months since the seizure and I was finally going to get my day in civil court, which my attorney, David Aughtry, and I had been long awaiting. The federal civil trial would be held at the Richard Russell Federal Courthouse in Atlanta, Georgia. I had served six months of my three year prison sentence. The civil trial would be held in the Atlanta, Georgia, Federal Courthouse.

On Sunday, the day before the civil trial in January 1989, I was to be picked up and transported to the Douglas County jail because that was the jail where I would housed during my trial. It had now been over three years since the IRS had taken all of my assets by force with armed government agents, with no proof, court hearing, or any type of legal proceedings.

I had a lot of apprehension about being picked up at Maxwell Federal Prison Camp in Montgomery and being taken to the Douglasville, Georgia county jail. This county jail is just twenty miles outside the Atlanta federal courthouse area and it was at last finally my time to have my day in court. To my surprise, I was put in leg irons and chains around my waist and placed in a van with other inmates. While I was sitting in the van, I asked the driver why the leg irons and chains since I was in a minimum-security camp with no fence. The driver told me the IRS had specially requested the leg irons and chains on J. K. Jones.

Intimidation only made me stronger because it reminded me of my days when I was abused by my daddy. The van had about five inmates from different camps going to Atlanta. We had to stop for a restroom break halfway there. I got out wearing an orange jump-suit with leg irons and chains and only looked straight ahead, but I could feel people all around us staring at us. I used my powerful mind to control my thoughts thinking I was still a child of the King of kings and nothing else matters.

When we got to the Douglas county jail, I was placed on the third floor because they housed different ages on different floors. It was very filthy, and I was put in an eight-by-eight cell with bars like a caged animal and had to sleep on the floor on a one-inch pad next to the urinal. The stench from the urinal took my breath away. I was sharing a cell with a murderer and another felon who had the only beds in the cell; the jail was full.

I used my powerful visionary mind to put myself to sleep, saying a prayer every night. I made myself think I was in a Holiday Inn for the first three nights, until I got a bed in a cell with bars. Fact is, if you can control your thoughts, you can control your circumstance, simple but true.

I was picked up early every morning by US Marshals who carried me to the Richard Russell Federal Courthouse and was put in a cell in Atlanta and they returned me to the Douglas County Jail every evening.

The two US Marshals were most kind to me and even bought my supper at a fast-food place every night before going back to the Douglas County Jail. They paid for these meals out of their own pockets, after they saw how the IRS had abused me in court. That was a real blessing, and I thanked them for their kindness. This again is great proof of how God works through other people. I could not eat the food at the Douglas County Jail because it looked and smelled like dog food. I gave my food to the other inmates.

I noticed each of the five days I was there on the third floor that a lot of the inmates would walk around in circles and the majority of them were smoking while walking in these endless circles. Most of them would just blankly stare at me as if in anger while they were circling. I truthfully think some of them were mentally ill. I just stayed to myself and read my Bible at night until lock-down and I fell asleep. I did this same routine each night I was there.

The lunch in the federal courthouse was very good, and I was dressed in a suit each day that my son Kenny had brought to me from Macon to wear in court. The suit was two sizes too big for me now, because while imprisoned I had lost forty pounds in six months.

My attorney, David Aughtry's opening statement was absolutely brilliant about the Constitution. For about twenty minutes in his opening statement, he fooled everyone in the courtroom; including even the Tax Court Judge Gerber, out of Washington, DC, because he was reading a constitution. David stated to the judge, "Your Honor, this Constitution I have just read to you is the Constitution of the Soviet Union!" This was a giant wakeup call for everyone in the courtroom. David then went on to say, "Stalin's Constitution of the United Soviet Socialist Republic actually guarantees greater rights and freedoms than our own Constitution. But, the real difference is not the words that we or Stalin chose: it is the life we breathe into those words."

In addition, David emphasized this because the IRS violated my constitutional rights from day one starting in 1982.

According to David, on the issue of whether to exclude all the evidence the IRS had obtained through deceit, "Judge Gerber originally wrote the decision to go our way, as I understand it, but ultimately altered it to say that allowing the exclusion rule in a civil case was too much of a stretch." The IRS's hand was caught in the cookie jar, and the judge says it was a "stretch"? With this being said here are the facts proven in my case in a federal court in Atlanta, Georgia in 1989:

1. IRS criminal investigator Gary Schwab and Cunnard went to see my former CPA Everett Flournoy, Jr., on another matter and Flournoy volunteered my personal financial information in 1982. Mr. Flournoy did this as an act of revenge because I had fired him. Schwab and Cunnard conducted a secret criminal investigation for 18 months. This is against my rights and the law and all parties involved were aware of this fact.

2. IRS criminal investigator Gary Schwab then sent a pregnant civil auditor Bonnie Waldrep to our daycare center at our home in 1982. She went there on the pretense that she was inquiring about the possibility of putting her newborn in our daycare center as part of the deceit. She worked in downtown Macon in the IRS office which was seven miles from our daycare center/home in north Macon and she lived twenty-five miles south of Macon in Warner Robins. The only reason that the IRS conjured up that idea was so that they could spy on our business and home in hopes of obtaining additional evidence against me. This was done at the direction of Gary Schwab who is a criminal investigator, giving instructions to a civil auditor which is against the law and the IRS policies. The IRS policy states there is not supposed to be any contact between civil and criminal agents. The law states that a civil agent must turn over any audit to a criminal

investigation once fraud is found. With absolute power the IRS does not even abide by their own laws. This was the second step that they used to violate me and my rights.

3. During the court proceedings, criminal investigator Gary Schwab testified in court that he had read a feature article about the new home I was building in the *Macon Telegraph* in 1983. After reading the article, he stated that he looked up my income for prior years and lied in an internal IRS memo that there were no criminal possibilities in my case. He knew that statement was a lie because the home I was building was valued at approximately $500,000 which would have required three times more income than reported on my previous year's returns. The reason that he lied was to use the civil audit to get more information to further incriminate me which is also against my Fifth Amendment rights and the law because at that time the audit was still being done under the guise of a civil audit, not a criminal audit. Just let me reiterate something at this point, I did not have a clue, and had not received any type of notification that the IRS was even looking at me then for any reason.

4. In 1984, I received a regular letter from the IRS stating that they were going to do a civil audit on me and that it would be handled via mail. So I was not alarmed or disturbed and simply gave the information to my accountant

to handle. I did not know that I should seek advice, or that I was in anyway needing to protect me or my family. I had no knowledge of all the corruptive activity going on against me mentioned in items 1, 2, and 3 above.

5. In 1984, my accountant Billy Lamb told me that the civil auditor Bonnie Waldrep wanted to meet with Grace and myself at his office. So Grace and I went and met with them and Billy told us that the IRS had found during their civil audit that we had actually spent $100,000 more on the home than reported on our returns and that they wanted an accounting and explanation as to where these funds had come from. I told him we had been saving for our home for years and we had just completed it. He told me that I had to get a new accountant. When we were leaving his office, Grace told me that the lady from the IRS looked very familiar to her. There was a good reason for that because she had been to our daycare when they first started the investigation on me and my business.

6. After the audit went on and on, I sought the advice and hired a local Macon tax attorney, Jay Hawkins to help me with the civil audit.

7. Civil agent Bonnie Waldrep called me at my store in 1985, and told me she was at my tax attorney's, Jay Hawkins office and that she needed to ask me a few questions. Ms. Waldrep drilled me over the phone for over thirty min-

utes about my intent and I answered all of her questions. After I hung up the phone, I got a real bad feeling deep down inside that I had incriminated myself on that phone call. So I angrily got on the phone and called my attorney, Jay Hawkins, and asked him why did I have to talk to the IRS woman and you on the phone instead of you speaking to her on my behalf, isn't that what I am paying you for? Jay told me that he was not in the conference room when she called me and that until I called him that he had no knowledge of the call. We both knew then that I had been tricked and deceived by the IRS and my rights had explicitly been violated once again.

8. Jay Hawkins was furious and Ms. Waldrep makes feeble attempts to say that there was a typographical error on one of the two powers of attorney and he had left the conference room to check on a correction when she called me leading me to believe that he was present for the conversation with me. This was an outright lie because she had been talking to him about me as a client of his at that time for one and a half years prior to this incident. He immediately asked her to leave his office.

9. Jay Hawkins then sent a letter to the IRS protesting this illegal act of Waldrep contacting his client without his knowledge or presence therefore breaking my rights. The IRS replies to his letter with a Circular 230 letter threaten-

ing that they would stop him from ever representing another client in an IRS case for the rest of his career if he did not cease and desist with the complaint. This is the way that the IRS uses their absolute power to control the tax payer and their tax attorney so justice cannot prevail. With absolute power comes corruption.

I am not an attorney, but if you read item 2 above about a civil auditor, Bonnie Waldrep, being pregnant and coming to my wife's day care center in 1982, pretending to have an interest in putting her unborn child in our daycare and not identifying herself as an IRS agent would be considered "silent misrepresentation or tionally misleading." Judge Gerber's later conclusion here, "We do not preclude the use of the exclusionary rule involving a Fourth Amendment right within the context of a civil case." Keep in mind this was two whole years before I was ever sent a notice concerning a criminal audit on me.

Actually, I heard from someone else after my civil trial that two of Gerber's fellow judges on the tax court told him that I was a "sleaze bag" anyway. I can only assume that these remarks came after something that had been written about me by Schwab was presented to the courts.

The merits of the case were that I was right, and it was proven the forces of evil, the IRS, did violate my Fourth, Fifth, and Sixth Amendment rights as if they did not exist. In reality, you have no rights in the IRS's world, and the federal courts in my case allowed the forces of evil, the IRS, to win by cheating.

I just pray these two fellow federal tax judges who proclaimed I was just "another sleaze ball" are alive today to read the real truth! I have been told by David Aughtry, that Judge Gerber is now retired. He is the judge who tried my case in 1989.

Just think, it took five years after the forces of evil, the IRS, seized everything I owned illegally, and then the IRS was ordered to figure out what I owed in taxes by a federal tax judge in Washington, DC. So this is justice? The IRS told David that my case was so complicated that their computers could not figure out what I owed them. Who is kidding who?

The IRS did everything possible to destroy me but could not go the extra mile and kill me. I know why; I was, I believe, protected by angels.

One thing that caught my eye when we were preparing to start my civil trial that Gary Schwab entered the federal court room to sit with Mr. Jorgensen and he was carrying all of my records in a cardboard box with Tide Detergent ads all over it. It was so unprofessional looking and to me disrespected the court.

When my civil trial ended in a week, exposing the corruption of IRS, I felt very good about the job that David Aughtry, my attorney, had done for me exposing every bit of the corruption that he could find so clearly and undeniable by all who heard it in my court trial that week.

I was at the mercy of the IRS. By the way, I do not believe that you will find the word "mercy" in their millions of words in the tax law books of the IRS that is approximately seventy thousand pages. Look it up!

After all it was James Kenneth Jones versus the United States of America!

In the world of prison systems, they are in no hurry to get you back to your home prison after you testify. So you drift from prison to prison up to six months. In my case, there is a huge difference from being in a minimum-security prison to a controlled prison level—two men to a cell, with bars, locked up like animals with another inmate. The only option I had was to pay extortion money of 2,700 dollars to the IRS to have two hacks in a van take me directly from Atlanta to Montgomery. Understand this is one way! Think about it, I could have hired a private jet for that kind of money, one-way, in 1989!

I had Kenny, my son, to pay the local IRS the extortion money that day. I was put in leg irons and chains with two hacks and of course no communication. I was taken to a level-four prison in Tuscaloosa, Alabama, by mistake, and they left me. I tried to tell the hacks I was wearing green and supposed to be in Maxwell AFB Prison Camp. All federal prisons I knew of wore different colored clothes. The hack told me to shut up and get in the small room of thirty men. I went in and cupped my head down in my hands and started to pray, "Lord, please get me back to Maxwell in Montgomery!"

About ten minutes later, a hack came calling JK Jones saying, "You are in the wrong place, go with these people." The two hacks put me in leg irons and chains around my waist and put me back in the van. We went to a Burger King as soon as we left the prison. They left me locked up in backseat of the van while they went inside and ate but brought me back a hamburger and a drink. I had to eat like animal with the chains on my body while riding back to Montgomery. I had to pay ten dollars a mile (or twenty-three dollars a mile in today's world), a pretty hefty price for a hamburger and a drink and a ride from Atlanta to Montgomery by the IRS.

The IRS never had a clue that the more they did to destroy me that it made me a stronger man. I have to say I was so happy to see Maxwell AFB after seeing a real lockdown prison with two twelve-foot fences and being in very close contact with real criminals that day. The beginning of the end had started with the close of the civil case, and I knew that David Aughtry had done a great job exposing all of the corruption within the IRS.

Prison Pickup

Bring my soul out of prison, So that I may give thanks to Thy name; The righteous will surround me. For thou wilt deal bountifully with me.

Psalms 142:7

In prisons everywhere after you have nine months or less to serve there is one thing the prisons do to help you. Before getting out, you are allowed time out, and it is called "short-time." This short time allows the inmates in prison to have time out to get adjusted to the outside world again.

The first short-time limit is twelve hours. My two sons Kenny and Michael picked me up, and they drove me to see a movie and dinner. Not being a driver or a passenger in a car for some time, I told Kenny to slow down as he was scaring me. Kenny thought I was kidding, but I was not teasing with him when I demanded he slow the car down.

My sons then saw a daddy that they had never seen before: a broken man. I was no longer the man they knew as their daddy all their lives. I spent some time with them but had a hard time adjusting to the outside world at that time. I recall the feeling of wanting to be quite and bottled-up within myself because I had been stripped of my self-esteem.

As my sons drove off leaving me at the camp, I had tears in my eyes. I loved them very much, and I knew that the stores were going downhill very fast. I knew there was nothing I could do for now but pray. The next day I went back to my normal prison routine.

On my second short-time out, they allowed me twenty-four hours. It was a real break to have some time with my sons. I actually spent the night in a motel there in Montgomery. It was a real pleasure getting to spend that much time out of there and with them; it was September 1989.

I came back in really good spirits, as I knew it would not be long till I got out of Maxwell AFB Prison Camp. Upon my return that early Sunday morning, the camp had Charles Colson of the Watergate scandal come to preach to the inmates. He had served his prison time there in 1976. He was saved while in prison and had become an ardent Christian and started the Worldwide Prison Fellowship Ministries, of which he was the chairman of the board, after serving his time. He had become a great man of God and has written many books. I was honored to meet him.

After he preached that Sunday, I walked up to him and got his autograph. Mr. Colson looked into my eyes and wrote a reference to the Bible: Phil 4:11-13 and signed his name on my church program. Mr. Colson had to be a man of God to know I had lost everything that this old world had to offer; but one fact remained true, I truly had more of everything I needed from this old world, because I had God. I ran back to my bunk and anxiously read it. The verses were perfect for my spirit at that point in my life.

Not that I speak from want; for I have learned to be content in whatever circumstances I am. I know how to get along with humble means, and I also know how to live in prosperity; in any and every circumstance I have learned the secret of being filled and going "hungry," both

of having abundance and suffering need. I can
do all things through Him who strengthens me.

Philippians 4:11-13

GROWING BY DYING

"Verily, verily, I say unto you, Except a corn of wheat
fall into the ground and die, it abideth alone; but if it
die, it bringeth forth much fruit. He that loveth his
life shall lose it; and he that hateth his life in this
world shall keep it unto life eternal," John 12:24-25.

Jesus speaks in these words to show the benefit of his
death. Jesus also speaks of what it means when he says
"Follow me!"

There is a spiritual reality and paradox here. When we
die to our self centeredness, our worldliness, we can
begin to grow and become fruitful. If we work for our
own fame and gain we may succeed. That road leads to
self glory and it's end. If we surrender ourself to God
and the glory of God, God will lead us to success in
God's way. That road leads to life and growth and
fruitful people and communities.

Today's program is a living epistle of what can happen
when we believe this paradoxical truth. Most of the
people here know what it means to die in certain degrees.
When that "little death" becomes a burial into Christ we
begin to discover how we grow by dying.

I hope that today's program can generate hope and faith
and love as it gives glory to the God who alone can give
life and lead to life.

I had it all and lost it all, but I did know the difference,
for I was blind and now I could see because God had
opened my spiritual eyes!

I still keep this well-worn autographed program
from Maxwell AFB Federal Prison Camp in my Bible
today, twenty-one years later. I keep it there to remind
me how far God has brought me from that despair
and from the lowest moments in my life to where I
am today!

I now use this worn, ragged-edged program that Charles Colson autographed when I give my testimony at churches and the Macon Rescue Mission. I serve on the board of directors of the Macon Rescue Mission and have served in that capacity for ten years now. This voluntary job allows me to give hope to the less fortunate; I was one myself, twenty-four years ago. I know Jesus Christ is real. He is alive and the hope of the world!

Mr. Colson is a real man of God. I will never forget the piercing eyes he had and the way he looked into mine. I truly believe the old saying that you can read someone's soul through their eyes, I know he did mine that day in 1989. I knew that victory was very near! Once again, God had used someone else to renew my hope in Him!

Free at Last

On December 20, 1989, I was granted an early release. I was one of the three inmates that the warden had picked out of fifty to have an early release for good behavior to be home in time for Christmas. I was so surprised when Mr. Seifert, the warden, called me to his office over the PA system. I had never seen him in the eighteen months I was there. By the grace of God my dream had finally become a reality.

Mr. Seifert told me that I had been a good inmate, and he was going to give me an early release to be home for the holidays. I can't tell you how I felt going back to my bunk. I told my seventy-two-year-old Christian cellmate friend that slept on the top bunk that I was leaving, and he began to cry. He told me how much he would miss me as a friend in Christ, and I really felt sorry for him as he was also there for tax evasion.

I did not tell anyone but Pam my bookkeeper about my early release because I wanted her to pick me up and it to be a surprise to my family.

I got home about 10:00 p.m. that night, and I went to my home on the lake where my son Michael was living while I was in prison.

I truly felt like a fish out of water. The first family person I got to see was my youngest son, Michael. It was so funny when I saw Michael, because he said, "Daddy, tell me you did not break out!"

I said, "No son, I got an early release." We both had tears in our eyes and hugged each other, because I was finally reunited with my family. This was a magic moment that I will never forget. We were finally united. We talked for a while, and Pam then took me to the halfway house in downtown Macon across from the Medical Center.

The halfway houses across America are the places you go to live to get adjusted to the outside world after your prison time. They also assist you in job placement. Prison life is a lifestyle that takes a heavy toll on you mentally and emotionally.

It is a well-known fact that in America we have a 70 percent return rate to prison. It is also a fact that America has the highest rate of incarceration per capita in the world. During my prison term, the prison system had about nine hundred thousand people incarcerated compared to about two million folks now.

Clearly, we are failing as a nation, and to put it bluntly, the trend started when we took God out of our classrooms across America in 1962.

The next day, I totally shocked my brother Harry and my son Kenny when I came walking into the store. Although, it was a day of glory, because I was a free man to some degree, something was wrong deep down inside of me. I was a broken man, for this ordeal had gone on for almost three and a half long years now, and

I did not see an end in sight. I still had the full weight of the government on my shoulders. Also, no decision on my civil trial had come down even though it had been over a year. I knew my attorney David Aughtry had exposed corruption within the IRS, but there was no ruling, so everything was still in limbo.

The first thing I did was take the little cash I had left, which Kenny had saved for me, and I took my two sons shopping at Macy's at the Macon Mall and bought clothes. It felt so good to do this because it had been years since we were able to buy anything. We were just that broke, and no one ever knew this but the three of us. I think we spent about a thousand dollars that day. We had bonded as one forever.

I started having nightmares and waking up in the middle of the night while in the halfway house mainly with fear about going back to prison. Here again Satan is always around in your weakest moments and tries everything to keep you stifled and steal the peace that the Lord gives you.

The first few days, I began to check the financial records to find out that the stores had declined from $2.2 million to $1.1 million in sales during the time I was in prison. The stores were ninety days behind on all the vendors, and I found over twenty-five thousand dollars of dead stock that had not been returned for repair in the back of the store. I had to throw all that merchandise away because it was out of the warranty period for repairs. New stock was given for need of repair inventory, thereby creating all of this as a complete loss of revenue.

Actually, the stores were in a free-fall the whole time I was gone. Plus the forces of evil, the IRS, were still forcing me to pay 5 percent of all gross sales on an alleged tax bill for a total dollar amount that had never been determined. It had been three and a half years of collecting, and the IRS knew they were breaking my back. The IRS was doing all they could do to destroy me and take me down financially.

One day Kenny and Michael asked me, "Daddy, who is the boss?"

I said, "I don't know!" I had to be honest with myself, and I was not stable enough mentally to restart my life and the massive rebuilding of my stores that was needed. I did not have the money to hire anyone for this responsibility.

The eighteen months in prison had taken a heavy toll on my mentality. I had gone from being a man that did not take orders from anyone, to a man going into prison humbled down to "a nobody" without a name and only a number. I had begun to lose what was necessary to survive. The one keyword was hope. I knew if I lost hope, everything would go down, and the forces of evil, the IRS, would win.

The worst thing to be without is hope. I got to thinking a lot about the one thing I still had. I had faith. Faith is the substance of things hoped for, the evidence of things not seen. I also remembered what Kenny had said to me, "Daddy, only God can help us now!"

While in the halfway house, I met up with the infamous IRS number one tax evader. He was infamous for leaving the country and not paying his taxes before he was sentenced. His actions really hurt me because the IRS blamed me for his sins. I had never met this man.

I heard his name many times by the IRS and in the news two years prior to my troubles with the IRS. The IRS acted as though I had serious money like he did. I often asked the IRS what this person had to do with me. The IRS never answered my question, and why should they? They do not have to answer to anyone. The fact is my story was so different from his because my assets could not be moved out of the country. Here again, the IRS has no common sense.

One night we were talking at the halfway house, and everyone was sitting around watching TV and introducing ourselves and he introduced himself to me.

I said, "I finally get to meet you; you have caused me so much trouble!" Unbelievably strange, but we got out the same week, put into the same halfway house and to add to that we were put in the same area with two bunks.

Now tell me that this was a coincidence? Tell me the IRS did not have our area bugged? This was no coincidence. The IRS was up to their old tricks.

It was revealed in 1989, in my civil trial by my attorney David Aughtry, that his case was the number one case dollars in middle Georgia in recent history in not paying his taxes. He said that my case was the number two case in dollars that did not involve narcotics, and it was not even a fraction of what they had done.

David Aughtry exposed their case in my civil trial and that the IRS knew my case was criminal in nature back in 1982. But the IRS disguised it as a civil case until 1986, proving that the IRS was absolutely wrong by comparing the two cases.

A New Start

Who also brings me out from my enemies;
Thou dost even lift me above those who rise
up against me, Thou dost rescue me from the
violent man.

2 Samuel 22:49

So the ninety-day period was up, and I was out of the
halfway house. I could now be a free man. I could now
live in my home at the lake. Having your freedom really
means more than you may think, for I truly believe that
freewill is of God. I now truly understand the story of
bondage and the biblical days of Moses.

It had been since June 27, 1988, almost two years,
and I had my freedom back. I still had to report to my
probation officer at the federal building every month.
This was to remind me I was still under the attorney
general's thumb for five more years.

I joined the city club, which was a private mem-
bers-only club. To my surprise, one time when I was
there Judge Duross Fitzpatrick walked up to me. He

had been the very fine Christian judge that sentenced me and also the one who reduced my sentence by six months.

When I saw the judge after I was out he always acknowledged me and asked me how I was doing. It made me feel that he respected me as a person when he spoke to me. I often saw him at Natalia's Restaurant, and every time he went out his way to say hello.

As the months rolled on, my mind began to heal by praying and using my visionary mind that God had given me from birth. I began to pray out loud constantly. Every morning driving to work, I specifically prayed to Jesus for what I wanted because the Bible makes it very clear to "Ask and Ye Shall Receive." I prayed for three specific things to happen:

1. I prayed for help to rebuild my business back greater than ever, in the name of Jesus.

2. I prayed to get a half-million dollar refund, in the name of Jesus.

3. I prayed that I would survive my battle against the forces of evil, the IRS, and I would give Jesus Christ, my Lord and Savior, all of the glory.

My attorney David Aughtry worked for the IRS prior to joining a law firm of fifty-two attorneys, and he knew how corrupt they were. He had absolutely destroyed them in court, exposing all the corruption, perjury, trickery, and deceitfulness in the Richard Russell Federal Courthouse in Atlanta, costing the US Government one-hundred thousand dollars for one week in 1989. Judge Gerber had made it clear to the IRS he would not come back to Atlanta to try Jones again.

I now had my head on straight, and the stores were now operating in the black. I was going to church, dating some, and my old self was coming back. But I did it in a humble way that was pleasing to God. I was still paying the 5 percent and paying some of the attorney fees, but I felt like I still had a problem with my self-worth and my self-confidence.

The most prized possession is integrity.

I had purchased a new car and the IRS had somehow heard about my purchase and called my attorney in Atlanta to tell me that I must sell the car. They said this because my tax case had not been settled. I told David to tell the IRS these exact words. I said, "I will not be selling my car as I am paying my taxes, end of story!" It felt so good to call the shots for a change, for it had been five long years. I had been through hell.

That made me feel so good again; somehow I was feeling my oats. I had taken on everything the IRS could throw at me and harm me with and had done my prison time. By the grace of God, I had survived.

I felt that indeed "Victory in Jesus" was coming soon. I was back to my old self again—large and in charge! The full weight of the government—the forces of evil, the IRS—had been on my shoulders almost five and a half years!

I got to thinking on the day I was sentenced to prison about what I had told my son Kenny—"Win I will, if the IRS does not kill me, so help me God!"

Reading the Bible makes it very clear there is a beginning and end to everything in life. I had begun to doubt because I had always been faithful in my beliefs. I knew it had to be Satan! The nightmare began October 20, 1986, and in five minutes my world was gone! Who was I to question the Almighty? If it started so quickly, why could it not end quickly?

Controlled Referral Program

The US tax court had now finally made a ruling on my case, it took so long for the ruling that I was beginning to believe it would never happen. They found as follows:

> Note: The legal opinion quoted in this chapter is from the following case: James Kenneth Jones and Grace A. Jones, et al., petitioners, v. Commissioner of Internal Revenue, respondent, United States Tax Court, 97 T.C. 7, Docket Nos. 4609-87, 4610-87, 31664-87. Filed July 3, 1991.

> Finally, we do not intend to condone any illegal or improper activity that may have occurred by declining to suppress evidence or otherwise sanction respondent in the setting of this case. Even though petitioners were unsuccessful in their motion to suppress, they have shown certain types of activity by respondent's agents which were either inappropriate and/or reprehensible.

Any attempt to conduct a criminal investigation under the guise of a civil examination would have a chilling effect upon the normal demeanor of the parties in civil examinations. As stipulated by the parties in this case, taxpayers are generally more cooperative in the setting of a civil examination, as opposed to criminal investigations where different procedures and rights are involved.

Initially, we point out that the majority of evidence tending to show that a criminal investigation was being conducted under the guise of a civil examination was circumstantial. Although we would not generally expect to see direct evidence of activity labeled as "deceitful," "misrepresentation," or "fraudulent," the cases in this area require clear and convincing evidence.

Additionally, an "affirmative misrepresentation" is prerequisite to a finding of a Fourth Amendment violation in this type of situation. In this case it would be difficult to decide whether Revenue Agent Waldrep had made a "silent misrepresentation [that] was both intentionally misleading and material."

In this case no inquiry was made and it is likely no explanation was expected by petitioners as evidenced by their cooperation with Revenue Agent Waldrep.

Finally, we do not intend to condone any illegal or improper activity that may have occurred by declining to suppress evidence or otherwise sanction respondent in the setting of this case.

Even though petitioners were unsuccessful in their motion to suppress, they have shown certain types of activity by respondent's agents which were either inappropriate and/or reprehensible. Although we do not extend the holding of *Tweel* to this civil case, *Tweel* also stands for the proposition that the Commissioner's agents are expected to deal in an honest and forthright manner when acting in their official capacity and may not abuse the power of their positions by deceiving a taxpayer in order to gain access to that taxpayer's files. See *United States v. Centennial Builders, Inc.*, 747 F.2d 678, 682 (11th Cir. 1984).

A number of facts are most troublesome. For example, Revenue Agent Waldrep's actual motives may have been revealed by her repeated (and successful) attempts to question Jones without the assistance of his attorney. Waldrep's actions in calling Jones from his attorney's office and implying that she was doing so with his attorney's consent and in his attorney's presence are reprehensible and, in the setting of this case, provide strong evidence of the deceitful nature of the agents' activities. Waldrep's excuse for her actions (that a typographical error rendered petitioners' personal power of attorney invalid) is a feeble and insincere attempt to legitimize her actions. Once access to Jones was terminated, Waldrep, without delay or further investigation, referred the case to CID for a criminal investigation. Although we have found it unnecessary to conclude that petitioners' rights were violated, it is evident that this was a close question and that it could have been decided unfavorably to respondent.

To reflect the foregoing,
An appropriate order will be issued.
Reviewed by the Court.

NIMS, CHABOT, PARKER, HAMBLEN, COHEN, CLAPP, WRIGHT, PARR, RUWE, WHALEN, and HALPERN, *JJ.*, agree with the majority.

KARNER, SHIELDS, SWIFT, and JACOBS, *JJ.*, concur in the result only

BEGHE, *J.*, concurring: This Court, having no general supervisory authority over respondent's operations (see *United States v. Payner,* 447 U.S. 727, 731, 737 (1980)), has traditionally refrained from trying to tell him how to do his job. However, the misconduct of respondent's agents in this case has been so egregious that I feel compelled to urge respondent to take some action, if he has not already done so, to reduce the likelihood of comparable misconduct in future cases.

CHABOT and COLVIN, *JJ.*, agree with this concurring opinion.

One day, in February 1992, I got a phone call from a local Macon IRS woman that wanted to meet with me at the store. She was very nice to me on the phone, which really surprised me. I agreed and was cordial. She began very nicely by telling me that the IRS would drop everything and would release all liens against me and my stores and set me free, if I would settle everything with them in full. I was in total shock! I told her thanks but no thanks. I had attorney's fees to pay, and I would never give up till the day I died. I told her to go back and tell her buddy Gary Schwab those exact words. She got furious and got up and left.

I felt deep inside that the IRS was now on the ropes. It had been three years since the civil case began. I think the IRS lawyer in Atlanta had put her up to try to settle my case.

It had been ten long years since my IRS nightmare had begun, even though I had I told my son Kenny, "I know the government is slow, but three years since my day in court? Why so long?"

The IRS lawyer also knew, according to David that if the decision went against us the case was going up to the Eleventh Circuit Court of Appeals and that was the reason the IRS wanted to end and settle with me. Jorgensen, the IRS prosecutor, had made the statement to my attorney to "hand Jones up on a silver platter, or we will audit your entire law firm of fifty-two attorneys." David called me and told me that Judge Gerber effectively sent a message to Mr. Jorgensen that he would not return to Atlanta to retry Jones and for him to settle the case immediately. David also told me that obviously the IRS had no desire to see the entire case laid out again in another court. The IRS felt it may not be as favorable to them.

Only then after seizure of all of my assets in 1986, prison time, money from my business every month, etc. did Judge Gerber force the IRS sit down until 11:30 p.m. at night with an accountant chosen by David Aughtry to determine just what I really did owe the government.

The enforcers of the law, who are supposed to be the authority, the IRS, are more corrupt than the people they say are corrupt!

But one of the real vindications came when the US Tax Court handed down its decision. Although the judges excluded the evidence that was obtained illegally from me, their decision called it "a close question that could have been decided unfavorably" to the government. One judge called the actions by the IRS reprehensible, and another called them egregious. What the judges did find, however, was precedent-setting.

I am speaking of agent Waldrep not informing me that the civil audit had started and that it remained as a criminal investigation. The court found:

> From the facts we find that the agent's failure to apprise the appellant of the obvious criminal nature of this investigation was a Sneaky Deliberate Deception by the agent under the above standard and a flagrant disregard for Appellant's Rights. The silent misrepresentation was both intentionally misleading and material.

The very next week, I get a call from my attorney in Atlanta, David Aughtry, telling me to come to Atlanta and that he had some good news for me. Kenny and I went to Atlanta to his office, and we were both very anxious and nervous. David greeted us with a big smile and said, "Let's go to the conference room."

The conference room was large enough for twenty people, and David began to tell me that I would get a substantial refund. He told me that he and his account- ant stayed up till 11:30 p.m. the night before with Jorgensen, the lawyer from the IRS, to try and figure out what was due me in a refund.

David went on to tell me the IRS did not make the minimum wage level on me after all of those years because I cost them so much time by refusing to quit my case and I interrupted David and said, "I just got to know. Give me a number."

David said, "About $383,000!"

I said, "Wow that is substantial!"

David said that I had done something that no one had ever done with the IRS. David went on to say since I refused to quit, the IRS had been forced to stop the Controlled Referral Program nationwide immediately. He told us that this was a huge decision for future tax- payers against the IRS using civil audits as a disguise for criminal cases.

I asked David a key question that did not make common sense to me. If Judge Gerber denied that my Fourth, Fifth, and Sixth Amendment rights were bro- ken, then why did the tax judges force the IRS to stop the Controlled Referral Program nationwide immediately? David said the Court essentially found that my rights were violated but that there was no real remedy.

David was really upset about the way the IRS seemed to be carrying out a vendetta against me. He said their vengeance against me was unlike anything he had ever seen or heard about. As for the lengths that the IRS went to try to destroy me, David thinks the IRS would say, "Don't confuse me with the Bill of Rights." It was like allowing a beat cop to run the DA's office. The government decided they didn't want to be bothered by things like the Fourth, Fifth, and Sixth Amendments. The government should not be stooping that low. And what did the decisions in my case mean to the average taxpayer?

This was a huge win for me and for all of the American taxpayers to stop the reckless behavior and unlawful program of using a criminal investigation under a civil guise. I am sure that the change of this ruling kept a lot of folks from experiencing the deceitfulness and corruption that was used on me is what he told me. David told us that this was a huge decision for future taxpayers against the IRS using civil audits as a disguise for criminal cases.

The IRS was told to immediately cease its national Controlled Referral Program since a criminal investigation should not be conducted under the guise of a civil examination.

I told David that this proved that the IRS was using a civil audit to disguise a criminal case against me by with the judges imposing no remedy against the IRS. In all reality there was no justice shown because the IRS has absolute power at all levels of the government.

I reiterated to David, "Please tell me I am wrong." David told me that someday I should write a book on this to expose the corruption.

I thanked David and asked how long it would take to get the money from them because we were dead broke. David told me he did not have any idea. Kenny and I drove home, and I was thanking Jesus for the victory and the fact He answered my prayers. The forces of evil, the IRS, had fallen to the King of kings.

David said of the decision that my refund of almost four hundred thousand dollars was substantial but not sufficient for what I had endured. According to him, the most important point was that my case killed the Controlled Referral Program that allowed the IRS to conduct a criminal investigation under the guise of a civil audit.

By the time we got to Forsyth, Georgia, I called Jay Hawkins, my local Macon attorney and told him my good news, and he exclaimed, "No way!" I assured him that it was the truth per David's meeting with the IRS and the letter received from them. Jay couldn't believe it. Jay told me there were only sixty-three people who had ever survived a jeopardy assessment, and I was number sixty-four.

To my surprise, the liens on my stores were released in a week, which Jay told me was completely unheard of. Because the IRS was so wrong about everything, they were going to do everything fast to get rid of me in a hurry.

Of course with absolute power, the IRS had almost 45 percent of the $383,000 refund paid as interest, so in turn I had to pay taxes on that money all over again, and the rest went to my attorney's fees.

DISTRICT COUNSEL
Internal Revenue Service
Southeast Region
P. O. Box 901
Atlanta, Georgia 30370
(404) 331-6243
(FAX) (404) 331-2761

February 16, 1993

CC:ATL-TL
WNTimm:fc.ltr.jon

David D. Aughtry, Esquire
233 Peachtree Street, NE
Suite 1400
Atlanta, GA 30303

Re: James Kenneth Jones & Grace A. Jones
       Docket No. 4609-87
       James Kenneth Jones
       Docket No. 4610-87
       Ken's Audio Specialties & Sewing Center, Inc.
       Docket No. 31664-87

Dear Mr. Aughtry:

Based on the computations completed by the Appeals Division and the executed Decision documents signed by you on behalf of the debtors on February 12, 1992, it is our opinion that the taxes have been fully satisfied as to Mr. and Mrs. Jones. We understand that there will be substantial overpayment and that you will formally request a set off of those overpayments to the corporate liabilities and only the difference refunded to Mr. and Mrs. Jones. We have this date requested that the Internal Revenue Service release all filed Notices of Federal Tax Liens and cease any further collection action with respect to these accounts as they have been full paid. We have contacted Revenue Officer Bush and requested that she institute the proper release of liens in this case.

We anticipate that once the Decision is entered and the Appeals Division makes the necessary adjustments in the account, that Mr. and Mrs. Jones, as well as the corporation, will begin to receive numerous adjustment documents. We request that once Mr. and Mrs. Jones and the corporation receive these various documents that if the resulting refunds do not match with what you believe to be the basis of settlement in this case that you contact Mr. Jorgensen of our office at which time he will meet with you and go over the actual transactions that have occurred based on the transcript. It is our understanding that probably the adjustments will take several months.

District Counsel IRS Refund Letter

Please note on this substantial refund letter that, based on the content of it, this reply was based on the executed decision documents on behalf of debtors (me) on February 12, 1992, and the letter from them is dated February 16, 1993. It took the IRS one year to get this letter out to my attorney on my behalf. It then took them another year almost to start sending the refund checks to me. Also, another thing to note is that all of the refund checks were dated November 23, 1993, which was nine months after the receipt of the substantial refund letter. It also took them fourteen months to send all of the checks to me. Go figure that one.

Copy of First Refund Checks

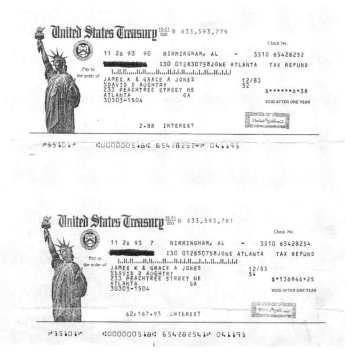

Copy of Second Refund Checks

My prayers were being heard; my probation officer called me and told me I was totally released from the US Government—two and a half years early. That meant I could leave the state and go to electronics conventions in Las Vegas. I was finally a free man again! The bondage of the government was over! Praise God!

I am just one victim out of thousands of people who have been destroyed or played as a pawn by them. I am poster child for tax abuse and the reason we need FairTax policies!

The IRS has absolute power, and now you know why so many American citizens commit suicide while fighting their battles with them. If we are a republic of the people, by the people, and for the people, we should not be in constant fear of any part of our government, and we must abolish the IRS and all of its corruption with it. The Fair Tax system is the only way. The current tax system is costing us 350 billion dollars a year. For this nightmare that nobody understands? This is nuts on all of our parts.

Jay Hawkins called me and told me the State of Georgia was asking for seventy thousand dollars more in state income taxes. I did get the money up in sixty days. I think the state was surprised, and frankly I was too! Praise God!

But the fact was that the IRS did go through with their threat in 1994. David would not tell me about it because he had to be very careful on discussing this subject matter. He was doing it all to defend my rights as an American citizen. So this is justice? The IRS goes after my attorney David Aughtry for defending my rights and exposing the IRS corruption and they proceed to audit all fifty-two lawyers in his law firm?

With absolute power, the IRS controls the taxpayer and his attorney with threats of circular 230, which bars the attorney from ever representing anyone before the IRS, therefore destroying his living. In my case, defending my rights and exposing the IRS corruption cost David's law firm dearly.

I hope someday to go before the Ways and Means Committee on the hill in Congress to tell my story so the world will know the truth and start a serious debate about FairTax.org policies and hope for the laws to be modified—also, why the forces of evil, the IRS, need to be abolished.

I have a whole chapter on why the fair tax will save America!

I truly believe my case is responsible and started the creation of the taxpayer's so-called "Bill of Rights" in 1997. The problem is the IRS has absolute power today and is back to their old ways, again conducting civil audits and criminal investigations at the same time without telling them about the criminal investigation. Same old tricks. The IRS is still above the law of the land and must be abolished. Today I have been told that there is a Supreme Court case by the name of Payner that allowed the IRS to use prostitutes to gather information unknowingly from taxpayers at our expense with no remedy against the IRS. So the question is when will the forces of evil, the IRS, be stopped? They will only be stopped if we repeal the Sixteenth Amendment!

Climb Back to Self-Respect

Jesus did not let him, but said, "Go home to your family and tell them how much the Lord has had mercy on you."

Mark 5:19

One problem I had was to forgive myself for what I had done to hurt my family. I love my family more than life itself. I knew that material things could be replaced but lives cannot. I had confessed my sins to God, and he had forgiven me, just as I had confessed to my family and won their forgiveness. This scripture relates so much too how I feel about how I hurt my family and thankfully how I had been forgiven by them and God for my sins:

He who conceals his transgressions will not prosper. But he who confesses and forsakes them will find compassion.

Proverbs 28:13

I got to thinking on the day I was sentenced to prison about what I had told my son Kenny, "Win I will, if the IRS does not kill me, so help me God!"

I was so blessed to have the love and respect of my two fine sons, Kenny and Michael, during this entire crisis. My sons had felt the pain that I had endured and supported me a hundred percent. They also went the extra mile and worked extra hours for several years and did what it took for the stores to survive without the pay.

Often, when I was depressed, Michael, bless his soul, would lift me up during my darkest hours, and he never knew it. He has that magic touch, just as today, for I have always been his hero as well as Kenny's. Michael makes you feel good by just being around him.

This gift that Michael has is evident today on our infomercials. He uses this special gift from God every day, preaching in church every Wednesday night service and Sunday services when the senior minister is out of town. Michael is the vice president of our company and has been doing our infomercials for ten years and ends each one with a verse from the Bible. We are so much alike in so many ways for he has my passion for life.

Kenny has the gift of patience, like his mother, Grace. Kenny has been blessed with a wonderful wife, Melissa, and they share a love as strong as the day they got married. Kenny only looks for the good in people and is a hard worker. Kenny is very smart and is the president of our company. Kenny's faith in me gave me hope in my darkest hours when he said, "Only God can help us now, Daddy," something that I will never forget. I will never forget that rainy night one week after the assault in 1986 at the car dealership in Forsyth, Georgia. Grace was crying like a baby and Kenny (21) was standing the rain, saying to me, "I love you, Daddy. Everything will come out fine, Daddy, because you are a winner."

I began to go to different churches over the years, and I built my business back to five million dollars a year. Then I had my first massive heart attack with nine bypasses in 1997.

Fact being that the stress of the IRS played a huge role in my heart attacks. I went to an herbal doctor from Rome, Georgia, and he knew nothing about me and told me that something real bad had happened to me in 1986 or 1987 because my body had stress all over my body functions.

The hospital staff told me they had never seen two sons that loved their daddy so much to stay with me twenty-four-seven by my side in the hospital. My sons did twelve-hour shifts in the hospital while I was there. The nurses told me that it was unheard of. In fact, when I got to go home, my sons spent every night with me for two weeks, within fifteen feet of me, until I got my health back. God had bonded us together forever.

At that time I did it all, including the advertising, ordering inventory, hiring, firing, so my boys were lost as to what the needs of the business were on a day-to-day basis. I then started to tell them how to do it all because I had the knowledge, and I knew that knowledge was power. I knew that one day my sons would have it all. I was a mentor to both of my sons, and they began to take control because I had to have nine bypasses.

I had been going to church and attended different churches for many years but had not found a church with the same spirit of Brother Mayo's Assembly of God church that I had grown up in and where I was saved.

> Worship the LORD with gladness; come before him with joyful songs.
>
> Psalms 100:2

In 2004, God in all of his glory led me to a church where I felt God's spirit, just as I had felt in the church I grew up attending. This is my church today, and it is Parkway Assembly of God in Macon, Georgia. Pastor Joe Williams Jr. is the senior pastor there and is also a well-respected attorney in Macon. The spirit he had within him and that was very obvious to me is what drew me to him, for I saw a true man of God and I desperately wanted that.

I felt right at home at this church and was really blessed every time I attended a service there. Being aggressive as I am, one day in 2005 I walked up to Pastor Joe and told him that he was so good that he should be on TV. I asked him that day, "If I produced and paid for the TV time, would you let me put our church services on TV?" I told him that there was not an Assembly of God church service on TV in the middle of Georgia.

Pastor Joe said with a smile on his face, "Yes, Ken, I would agree to that!"

I went on to tell him, "Well, Pastor, there is one catch to it, I want to hear some old-time gospel songs sung like I grew up with, because that is one reason that I come to church because I love the songs like 'In The Sweet By and By,' 'The Old Rugged Cross,' et cetera."

Then Pastor Joe said, "Okay!"

So in the twinkling of an eye, like in the Bible, I started the media services for the church in 2005 and continue to produce and air them. The result for the church has been an increase in attendance by 50 percent, but my personal goal is 100 percent. Pastor Joe Williams Jr. has become a great friend of mine. He has a real gift and is very blessed to have his wonderful wife, Becky.

Joe's daddy, Joe Williams Sr., later told me that my daddy went to the old Assembly of God Church on Houston Avenue in south Macon with him in the seventies. He told me that he often sat by him in church. Brother Williams said that my daddy would cry like a baby often and talked about his son Kenneth with him. He knew that we did not have a good relationship. Brother Williams said, "Ken, I did not put that together for some time since your daddy passed away so long ago. Ken, isn't it amazing that God led you to this church and that you are now producing and broadcasting our services some thirty years later? It truly is a miracle, and I know that your daddy would be so proud of you for being so successful as well." He said, "Your daddy really did love you." I was not aware that daddy went to the old Assembly of God church in the seventies till Brother Williams Sr. told me.

Pastor Joe is one of my best friends, and in the real world what really matters most is family and friends. Having a man of God in your life is very important in times of need, as you will need the prayers of many. As I have stated previously, there is great power in prayer.

You have to have faith in God for it to work for you. The real key to this whole story is I never gave up on Him. After all, the Bible is clear on faith. Jesus said, "We can do greater things than he." God states, "We are created in His image."

I give all the glory to Jesus Christ, my Lord and Savior!

IRS: Worse Than the Mafia

Even the Mafia has more morals than the IRS does. The Mafia does not go after the family but that is not the case with the IRS. The IRS froze a bank account of one of my relatives, and the first question the IRS asked of them was, Is J. K. Jones a relative of yours? It was a shame because the fact remains that they had absolutely nothing to do with my IRS issues.

Another instance that happened to me in July 1987 was Schwab came by my home one night about seven p.m. to ask me a question. I was in a much weakened state of mind because it had been about eight months since the IRS had taken all of my assets and my divorce was final, and my self-esteem was shot. He knew all of this. Plus he knew my attorney would not be at my home, but he came anyway. I answered the door when he knocked and he asked me if Michael, my son, was paying me any type of rent for living there with me. I told him of course not and he had not been as I had never charged my sons any type of rent fees ever. I found out in 1989 from my attorney David Aughtry that if I had of said yes then the IRS could have taken my stores and anything else I had and sold them because there is an IRS law that states if you have any other type of income that is not reported, then they can confiscate everything and sell it. My attorney told me that it could have been any amount, even $20 per week, and they could have taken my stores and sold them if I had any type of additional income. Wow, I am glad that since Schwab decided to ignore my rights again and come to my home at night while I was in such a weakened state and without an attorney that I answered the question correctly, not knowing that I did. I had absolutely no knowledge of that particular IRS law until my attorney told me about after I told him about Schwab coming to my home.

Another item in retrospect that I found out that Gary Schwab the CID Investigator did was in 2003, a customer that I had known since he was a young black man in the 1980s, came to the store. I had read about him and a high profile drug dealer in the newspaper in the early '90s. His name was Papa Wheeler, and at that time he had a car paint store in Macon. He told me that he wanted to speak to me in private, so we walked over by our service department, and I said, "Okay, what is it?" Papa said, "I have always liked you and I wanted to tell you something." He said, "Do you remember that tall big fat dude that was after you when you were in trouble with the IRS?" I said, "Do you mean Schwab?" He said, "Yes, that dude." He went on to tell me that Schwab had come to see him when he was in trouble with the law concerning drugs in the late '80s, the same time period that I was in trouble with the IRS, and Schwab told him that his problems would go away if he would testify that I was in the drug business.

I was stunned to believe the IRS would use extortion to try and destroy me completely. I asked Papa exactly what he had told Schwab, and he said he told him that he would not do that because he had never heard anything about Ken Jones being in any type of drug business. He went on to tell him that all he knew about me was that I was a good family man and that he was not going to lie about me. He said that Schwab got real mad and just walked away. I asked Papa why he had waited sixteen years to share this with me, and he told me that for years he had been very afraid of the IRS. Again, God was looking out for me and Schwab could not hurt me any more and he never knew it.

About two years later, I read in the Macon Telegraph that two men had come into Papa's home and shot and killed him in front of his eleven-year-old son. The rumor was he was going to testify real soon in Florida against another major drug dealer. About a year later, I read that his eleven-year-old son that had witnessed his daddy being shot and killed had been hit by a school bus and died as a result of his injuries.

Since Macon is such a small town I started asking people did you know Papa Wheeler and one day by the grace of God I met a man that came in the store that told me he knew of conversation between Papa Wheeler and the IRS man Schwab. He said he worked for Papa at that time and was waiting in car while the IRS man was talking to Papa. Papa told me the fat man was IRS man name of Schwab and asked him to lie about Ken Jones being in the drug business. He told me the IRS man offered him a deal to lie about Ken Jones. Papa told me he turned him down and thought it was real dirty in 1987 for Papa had bought car stereo's from Ken since he was a kid and liked him and knew he was in trouble with the IRS. Papa told me knew I was a good man and would not lie and the fat man Schwab got very mad at him. He told me he got into trouble later as a drug dealer and was was now a reputable businessman and christian.

So I have a person to back up my story. The Holy Bible is clear on this subject, be sure your sins found you out.

Fact is, our government has people working for the IRS like Gary Schwab will take any measures to destroy a person. So I am going to fast forward my story and tell you that the IRS promoted this evil man for what he did to me for you have to understand this is the culture of the IRS. This is a another reason America needs a Fair Tax system. Here again I was protected by God and never knew this till 16 years later.

Question, how many people's lives has this man destroyed under the power of the government? This brings up another thought now because the real issue is that I don't have any idea what CID investigator Gary Schwab put in his assessment of me that he presented to the tax judges probably why they told Judge Gerber that I was a sleaze ball, after all it is:

James Kenneth Jones versus the United States of America

No one who practices deceit will dwell in my house; no one who speaks falsely will stand in my presence.

Psalms 101:7 NIV

Further Harassment

About a year after the precedent-setting US Tax Court decision was handed down, my passion was back. I had taken on the most powerful government agency in our nation and had survived it all with God's help. My prayers to God had been heard and answered, and I felt my old self returning.

As I had told Agent Gary Schwab on that terrible day back on October 20, 1986, when he threatened my son Michael, "You can do whatever you want to me, but do not bother my family. What you people are doing to me is wrong, and I will never quit to the day I die, and that is a promise."

The secret to winning is never quitting.

During that terrible nightmare that took seven years of my life, I never had to file for bankruptcy, which I easily could have done. Bankruptcy could have relieved me of the taxes owed, debts to my vendors, and I could have lost it all. But I eventually paid every vendor, and my personal credit was never tarnished. In fact, I applied and got an American Express card a month after I got out of the prison.

In 1993 and in 1996, the IRS audited me again for six months, but I had no fear. I knew I had properly filed and paid my taxes, but they were still trying to intimidate me. My accountant and the IRS came to my office, and the agent asked me what kind of hunting camp I had around Talbotton, Georgia, about forty miles from Macon, in 1996.

I responded with anger in my voice, "I don't know why you people keep insisting I have another business or some type of hunting camp, what it is with you people?"

He said, "You also owe six thousand dollars on income because your business is paying for your health insurance."

I turned to my CPA and asked, "Is that true?"

He stammered, "Yes."

Obviously I was angered, but I asked the IRS Agent, "How in the world am I supposed to know all the tax laws when I am paying my CPA to know his job and he doesn't?" I turned to my accountant and said, "You're fired."

I then asked the agent what he meant by insisting that I had another business in Talbotton. He told me that he had examined all my telephone records in secret for the last six months, and I had made lots of calls to Talbotton, Georgia. I smiled in reply and said, "I'm going to tell you a little secret that will embarrass you. I don't have another business. On the side of Lake Tobesofkee where my house is located, the telephone service is not Southern Bell but a Reynolds phone company that is based out of Talbotton, Georgia, so all those calls are to my home."

Now, Mr. IRS man, have you people ever figured out that I just might be a hard worker and smart enough to earn good money even though we live in middle Georgia?

I told the IRS man that I would pay whatever he said I owed the IRS and to just send me a bill. About a month later, I received a letter from the IRS saying I didn't owe any money. So I haven't heard a word from the IRS for fifteen years.

David told me he had never met a man that would not give up and a man that never wavered. David said I should write book on this event.

David has been the main speaker at CPA conventions around America, and he tells of the man that owns a stereo store from Macon, Georgia, who absolutely refused to quit. He also tells them that I never lost hope and my case forced the IRS to stop the Controlled Referral Program nationwide. Fact is it was Jesus Christ, my Lord and Savior, and my two great sons that gave me the hope I needed in my darkest hours.

Why a Fair Tax system will save America!

The Fair Tax system should be called the common sense tax in my opinion. Neal Boortz, a national talk show host out of Atlanta, along with a former congressman John Linder from Georgia, wrote a book about it several years ago, which started the movement.

The part I love the most is that the Fair Tax gives the power of our own money back to the people. Money is power, and the Washington crowd will fight us tooth and nail to keep the power of our money in their hands.

The Fair Tax system is nothing more than a national sales tax. It is completely transparent, and since the American economy is based on 70 percent consumer spending, this is a great way to collect taxes.

Remember it is always easy to spend other people's money, which is rightfully ours. Our taxes affects every aspect of every American at every level and all the special interest groups, all loopholes for the rich will be gone with this system. The biggest bonus of all is that no one will ever have to file another tax return again, ever!

Also another good part of this Fair Tax program is that the low-income people do not pay any taxes. Now the low-income people pay taxes through payroll taxes if they are employed. Under the Fair Tax program the low-income people will receive a monthly prebate for necessities. Here are the facts, and you must get involved to save America and get our republic back in control of the people as was written by our founding fathers in our Constitution.

I have listed a general outline of the program as I know it:

1. Keep your whole paycheck. Everything like federal, social security, Medicare, Medicaid taxes, will no longer be deducted from your check. This program will do away with the corporate taxes. It will also do away with the death taxes, which by the way is double taxation because taxes have already been paid on those moneys at least one time. Thousands of families have lost their businesses in the last fifty years just in order to pay the death taxes, which are wrong in my opinion.

2. The Sixteenth Amendment would be appealed, and the IRS would be eliminated. Praise God! The forces of evil, the IRS, would no longer be a tax burden to the tax payers.

3. Everyone, even the Washington crowd, states the IRS tax code is a nightmare, full of special

interest, and no one understands 70,000 pages, but with replacing it with the Fair Tax system there are only 133 pages. The IRS code has six million words in it.

4. Low-income/poverty level people will get a pre-bate of between four to five thousand dollars for necessities, which is free money. In fact, everyone will get a pre-bate up to the poverty level as a given tax incentive. This is better than today's 15 percent federal tax plus, 7.2 percent social security tax system. There are special amendments already built into the system for low-income people for food, clothes, and transportation necessities.

5. The IRS estimates there is an underground economy of one and a half trillion dollars, and this would be eliminated. It may be a lot more. All people who are buyers, like illegals, drug dealers, you name it, would pay their fair share, at the cash register. Everyone pays twenty-three percent and walks away, end of story.

6. The IRS collected 2.2 trillion dollars in 2010, but it took approximately 350 billion of these dollars for IRS compliance, which included taxpayers and IRS procedures support to do this, which is a waste. This could be moneys that could be used to pay down our national debt. The building industry would go through the roof, for I have been told there is a 22 percent hidden cost in the homes and buildings.

7. America will have approximately forty-one million new taxpayers. Approximately forty-one million people, maybe more come to visit America each year and they would pay twenty-three percent on all goods and services. The total tax dollar amount that this will bring into our country is an unknown factor, but it will be an incredible amount, I believe. Today, the IRS laws are forcing our major manufacturing plants to keep their money overseas trillions of dollars, and it would come home if the Fair Tax system would become law.

Look where we are today.

With the Fair Tax system, just think about how easy it will be to pay your house note, bills, rent, etc. because you will have your whole paycheck. Also, when you die, your family will receive what is rightfully theirs since it will eliminate the death tax.

I have a strong passion for the Fair Tax Bill that is in the Senate today, HR 25 and S-13 bill of 2011 by Senator Saxby Chambliss of Georgia and Congressman Ron Woodall of Georgia, whom I know. Since I own two electronics stores and a music store and now have been in business for thirty-four years, I have a unique perspective as a business owner.

There is a little known secret the IRS made into law that put a heavy burden on our factories in 1976. This unfairly taxed both sides and collected very little in revenue, but did huge damage to our economy and factories. The little known law started to tax our goods we made in America on both sides, here and overseas, making our factories noncompetitive to other countries overseas. It only gave American factories two choices, our factories had to build factories overseas or hire a company to sell our goods overseas. You can see this when our America had our first trade deficit and I think you will be surprised. Folks, do not blame our companies; blame our government with no common sense! If logic did prevail congress would stop this IRS law today.

America started making us a cashless society about twenty years ago. The fact is about 97 percent of all our sales receipts in my retail world comes in the way of checks, credit cards, and zero-percent financing. Profit margins are about 1 to 3 percent in my highly competitive electronic business.

I would go one step further in the Fair Tax bill and collect all moneys that go in the banks from the businesses for taxes the very next day. This is a simple and transparent way to handle it. It would save over $350 billion dollars a year in compliance cost to the American people, so why not? The reason it is not liked by the majority of the folks in our government is because of a simple fact, if you control the money, you control the people, and they have that now. The last ten years our national deficit has tripled. Also, just think about the estimated IRS trillion dollars plus underground economy would be collected when people buy new goods and services. Illegals, drug dealers, etc., everyone pays and that is why it is called a fair tax.

The building industry is so important to America's economy that I would exempt the building industry for five years since it has been so depressed for at least five years. Once the industry is on its feet then it could be established at a 10 percent rate on new homes and a 5 percent rate on used homes.

Governor Mike Huckabee is my hero because he often says, "Do you think drug dealers file tax returns?" He wants to abolish the IRS as I do because I am the poster child for such an action. The fact is a lot of folks do not file tax returns because they are so complicated and you can go to jail for perjury like me. Everyone needs to read the bottom of their tax returns below the signature lines. In 2008, America had fifteen million more tax returns than 2007. Why? It was because President Bush offered $600 for every individual that filed a return.

Is our tax system today fair? It is not fair when 47 percent of Americans pay no federal taxes at all.

I think that if you are in the top 25 percent of folks paying 86 percent of all federal taxes, you must accept the fact you are the statue and the government is the pigeon.

Will Rogers, a US humorist in the 1930s, relates my feelings about the mess we have in Washington today. Here are some of my favorite quotes:

a. Ancient Rome declined because it had a senate, now what's going to happen to us since we have both a senate and a house?

b. On account of being a democracy and run by the people, we are the only nation in the world that has to keep a government four years, no matter what it does.

c. Be thankful we're not getting all of the government we are paying for.

d. The income tax has made more liars out of the American people than golf has.

Visit Fairtax.org and read and study all that is on their website. You will see that it is in your best interest to take home your whole paycheck. Time is right for a change to the way of collecting taxes, a transparent way. This would be a very fair way to collect taxes and give you control of your own money to spend as you please without government intrusion of your privacy.

Fair Tax Versus Flat Tax

The 20 percent payment on this system would really hurt the low-income people and the middle-class people tremendously. They have had this system in Asia for years, and it does not cover the tax cheaters, nor protect your privacy.

How the Fair Tax system benefits America:

1. It will grow our economy by leaps and bounds. It will also greatly increase our global competitiveness. It will create lots of jobs because small businesses and corporation will know what their tax basis will be now and in the future, creating certainty in the market place.

2. Encourages and grows the American work ethic because you will be bringing home your whole paycheck.

3. For the first time in history, America will be a tax haven for business and for jobs. The current stranglehold of the laws and administration will be gone.

4. It will make the United States an investment refuge with tens of trillions of dollars returning to our shores that corporations and individuals have been stowing away in offshore accounts or investments in other countries.

5. It will reduce our trade deficit by making our products competitive with our foreign counterparts. The IRS started taxing on both sides of goods back in 1976, making America a noncompetitive vendor in the marketplace.

6. Huge unknown underground revenue would become void basically and would even out the tax burden with everyone paying their fair share.

7. Fair Tax National Retail Tax is transparent, simple, and will basically rid America of tax cheating because everyone buys clothes, food, cars, TVs, services, etc. used goods are excluded.

8. The cash register is your tax return and all states would collect the taxes.

As a tax cheater myself in the 1980s, I admit that I was dead wrong and I have a unique perspective as to why people cheat on their taxes today:

1. Most Americans feel that other Americans are not paying their fair share of taxes. This is by far the number one reason.

2. A lot of Americans do not feel that America should be in wars all around the world and attempt to be the policemen of the world. Since they feel that way, they do not like our tax funds being used to fund the wars.

3. Fifteen percent of all Americans feel like it is not a crime to cheat on their taxes.

4. Also a good deal of Americans feel that we give out money through government programs to people who are not deserving or not qualified because they are allowed to receive the funding because they are lying about their situation.

5. The forms, laws, tax rates, and guidelines change on a yearly basis, and a lot of people do not file because they don't understand the forms nor the laws and the changes and do not want to spend money to have them prepared by a professional.

Folks, the fact remains there are only about 115,000 IRS agents in America, and the good news is that our government has established a taxpayers advocate group to help taxpayers in trouble, which is a good thing established sometime after 1997 after the taxpayers "Bill of Rights" was passed. I have been told that approximately four years after this law was passed that the IRS went back to their old ways. I pray not.

The IRS estimates that taxpayers like you and me that pay our taxes pay an additional $2,200 per year for the tax cheaters. This probably has you thinking, what is the real answer for America to correct this situation of non-taxpayers and cheaters? There is only one answer, and that is the Fair Tax system because it is transparent to all Americans. You can go to Fairtax.org and should be able to find information to address any concerns you might have.

There is no way to audit sixty million tax returns with only 115,000 agents. The only way to get all of the tax cheaters is at the cash register because we all as Americans have to buy goods and services. The big bonus in all of this also is that the estimated forty-one million foreign visitors that we have in the United States each year would become new taxpayers here that buy goods and services every year if we had the Fair Tax system.

It is just common sense, as where I live in Georgia I pay a 7 percent sales tax and think nothing of this when I buy anything.

Now think of it this way. If the State of Georgia billed me for my sales tax every month and had to hunt me down to pay my sales tax each month, just guess how hard that would be. It would be totally counter-productive, and there is no way that Georgia could hire enough people to collect the sales taxes from millions of Georgians. Also, how about the people who move around a lot? For all of the right reasons, the sales tax is collected at the time of purchase, which is simple and transparent.

This is my point exactly as to why we need to change our federal tax system to one that is a common sense system that is simple and transparent and easy to understand. It will collect the taxes at the cash register when you buy goods and services, and used goods are excluded.

Another interesting fact about our tax system set up as it is now, it invites crime in another sector of the tax preparers. A lot of the tax preparation firms charge a percentage of what your refund will be as their fee, thereby opening the gates for another form of tax cheating. There have been a lot of cases where folks have lost everything thinking they were using a legitimate tax preparer to find out that their taxes were not filed properly or deductions taken were ones that are not allowed. If this happens, you (the taxpayer) are liable for the taxes and interest/penalties, and the possibility of jail time as well as loss of assets happens all of the time. Usually the tax preparers who cheat in this case will serve prison time as well as penalties.

This will make you free to live your life as the republic we were founded to be over two hundred years ago, and when you walk away from the cash register you have filed your tax return. Did you know that Americans pay twenty-two billion dollars a year just to file their income taxes? A billion is 1,000 million dollars, and that is just for preparation fees. How much more food could you be able to put on your table, or how much more would you have to help someone, a family member or a friend in need, if you had those extra funds in your pocket? This giant expense would be eliminated off of the American people with the Fair Tax system.

Everyone would pay the same tax, just as a sales tax! Neal Boortz, nationally syndicated talk show host out of Atlanta, who happens to be another one of my heroes, has been wearing out the radio waves on this subject for years. But the fact remains that most Americans do not have a clue about the single most important issue to save America, including our congress.

A national sales tax, which is known as the "Fair Tax," needs to be addressed to stop tax cheating dead in its tracks. People who oppose the Fair Tax will say tax cheating will be rampant, but in my opinion the opposite will happen. States will only have to monitor businesses and most American businesses receive very little cash because credit card sales are now as American as apple pie.

Last year Senator Harry Reid of Nevada made a statement that got national attention when he stated on national news that our tax system was voluntary. Wow, I can only guess he has never worked and received a regular paycheck where the taxes are deducted from the money you are paid before you receive your balance of money minus taxes collected. I hate to tell him, but Mr. Reid, the system is not voluntary because the government has those funds deducted from your pay and sent to the US Treasury before you obtain your check.

The Fair Tax system would be voluntary because you only pay it when you buy goods or services on your own terms, spending your money as you see best for you and your family.

As an American, I truly believe that it is my responsibility and duty to pay my taxes. I love my country, and I was dead wrong for not paying my taxes. My family and I paid a heavy price for my sins. I have no ill will toward the IRS for the past, for the past is just that, the past. I know of no other country in the world like America where a man born to a poor family with only a high school education could build a multimillion-dollar business with only a dream and his visionary mind. Where else could a man rebuild his life and meet and shake the hands of President Jimmy Carter and President George W. Bush?

The Visionary Mind
Is Real!

> But if any of you lacks wisdom, let him ask
> of God, who gives to all men generously and
> without reproach, and it will be given to him.
>
> James 1:5

I have talked about the visionary mind throughout
the book that helped me survive the attack of the full
weight of the US government for seven years. One day
I looked at my eldest son Kenny and said, "The IRS
made a fatal mistake, the IRS did not kill me like the
Nazis did the six million Jews in World War II, so win
I will!"

This power within me is of God, and the majority
of people have no knowledge of it, even though they
may have used it and not even have known it. The
Holy Bible is full of men with the power of God with
visionary minds such as Moses, as one example. Some
examples of people with visionary minds that are using
theirs in the last one hundred years are Bill Gates,

Donald Trump, Thomas Edison, Warren Buffet, and Mark Zuckerberg.

Jesus is clear in the Bible about many wonderful things, such as "The Kingdom of God is within you."

God says, "You can do greater things than I."

God, in the Bible, says, "We are created in His image."

Take a moment to realize what those words the Holy Bible are saying to us, as this is a realization of God-power within you and your rights of dominion over your own body, your health, your prosperity, your business, and your environment.

This is a very real. In all reality, having a vision-ary mind makes dreams come true. It is a law of visu-alization. This law calls into being in the outer mate-rial world everything that is real in the inner world, if you will.

The keyword is the imagination of your goals by displaying pictures of what you desire. Vision (your inner being) idealizes it. It reaches beyond the thing that is desired and gives you the impulse vision and makes it real.

Make your mental image clear enough; picture it vividly in every detail. Believe in it, and your visionary mind God has given you will make it a reality, but you must not doubt. Vision without faith is nothing!

The Bible teaches to look upon God as three-in-one: the Father, the Son, and the Holy Spirit. We are made in His image as one, the subconscious as two, and the subliminal or the super-conscious mind as three, which I call the visionary mind.

The conscious mind is I see, I hear, I smell, I touch, I taste, and it controls your voluntary muscles and to some extent what is wrong and right. It is also is the watchman of the gate to your subconscious and super-conscious mind.

This is where the visionary mind kicks in. Since the conscious mind is the watchman at the gate, it is very important what you put before the gate to get to your super-conscious or visionary mind working.

If you put fear, worry, defeat, or even fear of cancer, or thinking you are a loser, at the gates of your mind that is exactly what you are going to get. The suggestions of disease, fear, or whatever penetrates your thoughts and your own beliefs of your mind make it a reality. It directs and controls every function of your entire body, and only you can dictate your negative or positive thoughts you put at the gates.

When I was growing up as a boy, I rejected the negative words of my daddy to me, for my mother always gave me loving, kind words and told me that I was smart and special. Daddy put me down, for he felt that made him a bigger man. I guess this was a factor of never being loved by his mother. He also never had a daddy growing up. I always chose to believe my mother that I was smart and special.

Mother always tried to protect me from the physical and emotional abuse of my daddy. I think in retrospect that is why I got a job at nine years old carrying people's groceries home for tips. I knew somehow, someway I would be my own man, as a boy. That driving force as I grew up, forced on me to be the man I needed to be to fight the forces of evil, the IRS, against all odds!

You see, the subconscious mind occupies the entire body, and when not opposed, it has absolute control over your heart, circulation, lungs, and all cell life. It perceives intuition and even receives intelligence and transmits to people that at a distance. The power of the subconscious mind is unlimited. An example would be, if you have ever driven home and do not remember how you even got there. Fact is, you had something in your conscious mind while you were driving while your subconscious mind drove you home. This all happened without any knowledge of your trip home in your conscious mind.

Faith and belief is there if you read twenty-third and ninety-first Psalms to show the power of God and His readiness to help you feed your needs. Be thankful, not for past favors, but for the granting of the favor you are now asking to be given!

Believe! Once the gates are open to your subconscious mind with prayers, you will indeed have what you have prayed for, and it shall be yours.

I used my visionary mind to defeat the IRS through the power of prayer and faith. I never gave up on my faith or hope. My mind was always thinking of victory. My attorney David Aughtry was a real blessing. He was a gift and not a quitter. Failure to me was not an option, and I made that clear to David. It did not matter what the cost to me, for I had already been dirt poor, and I was determined not to go back, so win I would.

Failure was never an option in my mind, and failure never entered the gates of my subconscious mind.

David knew I had a passion to win, and I believe he felt my passion. When it's evil versus good, good wins every time. David gave me the words of the forces of evil, the IRS. David had worked for the IRS for several years and was aware of their corrupt ways. David had no fear of the IRS, and I admired him for exposing the corruption of the IRS in my case. David had no idea that I had no fear of anyone or I that had been abused as a boy.

David did tell me later that he had never met a man that would not give up. David was aware I had two fine sons that supported me 100 percent. I believed deep inside I would not be denied victory, for I was a child of the King of kings.

I have always thought you are going forward or you are backing up. God gave us all a twenty-four-hour miracle powerhouse that stores all our thoughts from the day we are born. This is our subconscious mind!

There is an old saying, "What does not kill you makes you stronger." As long as things run smoothly, the life force sleeps, but there is a second wind that kicks in moments of great stress that calls for superhuman deeds. The medical field calls it glands, and they pump stimulants into your blood. I call it a resource without limits, no matter how big or complicated the problem, the God-given visionary mind kicks in, if you will.

The same inner being inside that controls our happiness and contentment in life or our struggles and our strife depends on how we think. This inner being can be our servant or our beast; it all depends on which one you feed.

My cardiologist, Dr. Kalli, in Macon told me just three years ago that he has only known two men in his twenty-eight years of practice that have used their mind to heal their heart, and I was one of them. I have had two massive heart attacks along with fourteen bypasses. I was given a 5 percent chance of living in 2006. I thank God every night before I go to sleep for my heart with no pain now.

Fact is, the mind is the most powerful part of our body, and I am living proof!

Know that you can do anything you wish to do, be anything you wish to be. The rest will follow.

> If ye abide in me, and my words abide in you, ye shall ask what ye will, and it shall be done unto you.
>
> John 15:7

Full Circle
Conclusion

Over the years I reinvented the store's product lines and added home theaters, HD TVs, turnkey media rooms, church audio-video systems, and offered in-store or in-home technical support in middle Georgia and shortened the name to Ken's.

God has led me in all of the directions I needed to go with the visionary mind he blessed me with to keep my business strong and viable through the good and bad times. I am always heeding to that inner voice that God gives us through His Holy Spirit. He has directed my path in the right ways, to help me in my business and in my personal life.

On that fateful day back in October 20, 1986, the most powerful forces of the US government, the forces of evil, the IRS, seized everything I owned illegally with armed government men. They forced me to pay 5 percent of all gross sales for all of those years with the full weight and power of the federal government for almost seven long years, but by the mercy of God I survived.

Even though my case started as a civil audit, and was handled that way for at least three years, I was never informed that it had been turned over to the criminal division, and I never received any correspondence from the IRS other than the letter received to tell me initially that I was being audited under a civil audit. I never once received any correspondence or visits from the IRS to inform me that I was being audited under a criminal audit. I did not know what was going on at all until the day of the assault, when they came armed with US Marshalls to take my businesses and all of my personal properties and goods away from me. I was never read my Miranda rights during the entire time of any of the proceedings, hearings, or the day of the assault. I am willing to take a polygraph on this statement, and I am sure the investigators with the IRS will not.

I have never sat down to calculate the total amount that I paid to the IRS in dollars, or the total amounts that I paid out during the assault to attorneys and accountants. I know that it is a huge amount of money, but somehow God always made a way.

The almighty IRS had jumped on a man that had been abused all of his life from when he was a mere boy by an abusive father. Raised up poor in the slums of Atlanta, with only a high school education, he had been saved and had the power of the Holy Spirit of Jesus Christ alive in his heart. God in all His mercy forgave him of his sins and led him to victory in Jesus over the forces of evil, the IRS. Just think, if God can do such great things for me, what he can do for you!

You have to have faith in Him for it to work for you. The real key to this whole story is I never gave up on Him because I believed in what I was taught in church, that all things are possible through God. After all, the Bible is clear on faith. Jesus said, "We can do greater things than He." God states, "We are created in his image."

God, as also stated in the Bible, works in mysterious ways, and when I strayed from Him, he brought me back into His folds. By going through all of this with the IRS, He led me to be a much better man and strengthened me in my relationship with Him, my family, and my friends. I was justifying my sins when I strayed from God, and this was his way of using something in my life to bring me to an utmost humbled stage where there was nothing left but Him to lean on. I can now truly say I am amazed by His love and I am thankful to God that he allowed me to survive this turmoil and grow so strong in Him. He is a kind and merciful God, because if he had allowed me to continue on my path of self-destruction, I would be without Him in my life today, with no hope. He definitely brought me back to Him in a full circle, and I praise Him for my life, my family, my friends, and my businesses that I have today.

As you will see after this final chapter, I had one more step that I wanted to accomplish before my life story is over, and that was to receive a pardon from my felony conviction. Our former Governor of Georgia that I know, Sonny Perdue, wrote a letter to the President of the United States dated November 14, 2008, asking for a pardon for me because of the mistreatment by the IRS towards me and the fact that I served my time and paid my dues. Also, you will see attached here where I did not receive an answer to this request until two years later, and my pardon was denied.

CHAMBERLAIN, HRDLICKA, WHITE, WILLIAMS & MARTIN

A PARTNERSHIP OF PROFESSIONAL CORPORATIONS

ATTORNEYS AT LAW

DAVID D. AUGHTRY
SHAREHOLDER
DIRECT DIAL NO. 404.658.5486
E-MAIL: david.aughtry@chamberlainlaw.com

191 PEACHTREE STREET, N.E. - THIRTY-FOURTH FLOOR

ATLANTA, GEORGIA 30303-1747

(404) 659-1410   (800) 800-0745

FAX (404) 659-1852

HOUSTON
ATLANTA
PHILADELPHIA

July 11, 2008

President George W. Bush
The White House
1600 Pennsylvania Avenue, N.W.
Washington, DC 20500

> Re: *In re James Kenneth Jones*
>   *Request for Presidential Pardon*

Dear Mr. Bush:

On behalf of Ken Jones, I would like to outline briefly (i) why the Tax Court concluded that the IRS treatment of Ken was "reprehensible;" (ii) how Ken actually overpaid his taxes; and (iii) what a remarkable model Ken represents as someone who overcame adversity, paid all real and imagined debts to society, and avoided being consumed by the resentment that should arise from the reality that those entrusted with enforcement of the law repeatedly perjured themselves, violated the Constitution, and, in contrast to Ken, never suffered any adverse consequences whatsoever for their actions. Due to Ken's persistence, the IRS dropped the "Controlled Referral Program" that the IRS frequently used to conduct undisclosed criminal investigations under the guise of a normal civil audit.

Incident to my representation of Ken before the United States Tax Court, we discovered that the IRS had engaged in what the Fifth Circuit referred to as "trickery and deceit" in *Tweel v. United States*, 55 F.2d 297 (5ᵗʰ Cir. 1977), by pursuing a criminal investigation under the guise of a normal civil audit. The attached Tax Court opinion tells most of the story. At every turn, the IRS sought to deceive and manipulate Ken and his representatives. One paragraph from the opinion captures many but not all of the disturbing events:

> A number of facts are most troublesome. For example, Revenue Agent Waldrep's actual motives may have been revealed by her repeated (and successful) attempts to question Jones without the assistance of his attorney. Waldrep's actions in calling Jones from his attorney's office and implying that she was doing so with his attorney's consent and in his attorney's presence are reprehensible and, in the setting of this case, provide strong evidence of the deceitful nature of the agents' activities. Waldrep's excuse for her

President George W. Bush
July 11, 2008
Page 2

> actions (that a typographical error rendered petitioners' personal
> power of attorney invalid) is a feeble and insincere attempt to
> legitimize her actions. Once access to Jones was terminated,
> Waldrep, without delay or further investigation, referred the case
> to CID for a criminal investigation. . . . (97 T.C. at 29-30)

The Tax Court opinion omits what, in my view, is the most disturbing fact. When Ken's tax lawyer in Macon (Jay Hawkins) called to complain about the agent calling his client from his office and implying to the client that he was present, the agent then threatened to revoke the tax lawyer's license to practice before the IRS under IRS Circular 230. Not long thereafter, the IRS resorted to a unilateral jeopardy assessment and seizure of Ken's belongings and accounts – a tactic designed to deprive Ken of his ability to defend himself. While that occurred prior to my representation, my understanding is that his representatives then pointed out that no grounds existed for a jeopardy assessment and it was withdrawn on the condition that Ken make monthly payments against the unproven tax liability.

The IRS reaped the rewards of using the civil audit deception in that Ken pled guilty to at least one criminal tax charge, served his time, and returned to Macon to rebuild his life. Ultimately, the IRS agreed that Ken overpaid his taxes and refunded the excess (approximately $400,000) to him.

I know of no better example of a man who overcame so much abuse, persevered so in rebuilding his life, and just refused to allow these injustices to divert his positive attitude from contributing to his community. A pardon of Ken at this stage should encourage others to redeem their lives in the way Ken has and inject some measure of justice for the reality that, unlike the IRS agents who subjected Ken to such "reprehensible" treatment, Ken alone overpaid his debt to society.

Please let me know if you or anyone in your office has any suggestions or questions I can address.

With highest respect, I remain

Sincerely,

David D. Aughtry

DDA:rfm
Enclosure
cc: Mr. James Kenneth Jones
84674.1
880114-000000:7/11/2008

STATE OF GEORGIA
OFFICE OF THE GOVERNOR
ATLANTA 30334-0900

November 14, 2008

Mr. Ronald L. Rodgers
Pardon Attorney
United States Department of Justice
Office of the Pardon Attorney
1425 New York Avenue, N.W., Suite 11000
Washington, D.C. 20530

Dear Mr. Rodgers:

Please accept this letter on behalf of Mr. James Kenneth Jones of Macon, Georgia. I know Ken personally, and I am writing on his behalf to request a Presidential Pardon for his 1988 plea of guilty to two counts of violations of tax laws, specifically (1) making a false and fraudulent individual income tax return for 1981; and (2) making a false and fraudulent corporate income tax return for the taxable year ended April 30, 1983. *See Jones v. Comm'r of Internl Rev.*, 97 T.C. No. 2 (1991).

Two facts are most striking in Ken's appeal for a pardon. First, even in the light of the facts leading to his plea, Ken is clearly remorseful. His remorse is particularly compelling given the United States Tax Court's conclusion that Ken was subjected to "intentionally misleading and material" misrepresentation and a "sneaky deliberate deception by the [I.R.S.] agent." *Jones*, 97 T.C. at 23. Specifically, an agent investigating Ken called from Ken's attorney's office. The agent spoke with Ken, *ex parte,* and he led Ken to believe that his counsel was present in the room during the conversation. While the agent's conduct does not excuse the underlying facts of the case, it does show Ken's ability to accept his guilt and not blame others. Most importantly, Ken has never had a blemish on his record since serving his time, and in fact, the I.R.S. deemed that Ken overpaid taxes by an amount of approximately $400,000.

Second, Ken has the overwhelming support of his community. As evidenced by the letters of reference, he is very involved with several aspects of civic life in Macon. His "Guns for Tunes" program, which trades a car stereo for the trade-in of a firearm, has proven successful further and demonstrates Ken's commitment. He truly is a man who has served his debt to society and worthy of pardon.

Saved by the IRS

November 14, 2008
Page 2

Ken recognizes his errors, served his time and is now working to improve the lives of Americans. He asked my help not from bitterness, but from a true desire to remove the blemish on his record created by acts committed over twenty-five years ago. I can think of no reason to deny Mr. Jones his request for a Presidential Pardon, and I hope you agree.

Sincerely,

Sonny Perdue
Governor, State of Georgia

SP:jb

cc: The Honorable Janet Creighton

191

Ken Jones

Office of the Pardon Attorney

Washington, D.C. 20530

NOV 30 2010

Mr. James Kenneth Jones
125 St. Martinique Place
Macon, GA 31210

Dear Mr. Jones:

Your pardon application was carefully considered in this Department and the White House, and the decision was reached that favorable action is not warranted. Your application was therefore denied on November 23, 2010.

Under the Constitution, there is no appeal from this decision. As a matter of well-established policy, we do not disclose the reasons for the decision in a pardon matter. In addition, deliberative communications pertaining to agency and presidential decision-making are confidential and not available under existing case law interpreting the Freedom of Information Act and Privacy Act. If you wish to reapply for pardon, you will become eligible to do so two years from the date on which the President denied your petition.

Sincerely,

Ronald L. Rodgers
Pardon Attorney

My prayer is for this book to touch the lives of many and bring hope to all that need God in their lives today.

I would like to reiterate that the IRS broke my Fourth, Fifth, and Sixth Amendment rights and the tax court judge did me wrong, in my opinion because the judge forced the IRS to stop the Controlled Referral Program. If my rights had been proven not violated then he would not have stopped this program. Also I am so thankful that God allowed them to refund the moneys that they did. I will never feel as though I knew the correct amount owed to them and that I also know they were probably overpaid, but God saw me through all of this and hopefully this book will help someone avoid what happened to me.

My two great sons, Michael (left) and Kenny

I am so thankful from the bottom of my heart and soul for God's forgiveness and his rich blessings he has poured out on us since I have rededicated my whole life to Him. We have been continuously blessed by God and have been able to expand our businesses tremendously since that fateful day in October 1986. I have continued to be faithful to God and will do so until the day I die and go to meet Him. Praise and all glory are not by my accomplishments, but all due to God and to his ever-enduring, forgiving love and forgiveness. If we are faithful to God, he will be faithful to us. Amen!

I could not be defeated by the forces of evil the IRS, for if God is for you, who can stand against you! So, I was indeed Saved by the IRS!

I give all the glory to Jesus Christ, my Lord and Savior! Amen! Amen!

Ken's Macon Store
www.kensonline.com

Ken's Warner Robins Store

Ken's Pro Sounds